# Evaluating Research in Academic Journals

## A Practical Guide to Realistic Evaluation

### THIRD EDITION

Fred Pyrczak

California State University, Los Angeles

**Pyrczak Publishing**

P.O. Box 250430 • Glendale, CA 91225

"Pyrczak Publishing" is an imprint of Fred Pyrczak, Publisher, A California Corporation.

This edition was written in collaboration with Randall R. Bruce.

Although the author and publisher have made every effort to ensure the accuracy and completeness of information contained in this book, we assume no responsibility for errors, inaccuracies, omissions, or any inconsistency herein. Any slights of people, places, or organizations are unintentional.

Project Director: Monica Lopez.

Cover design by Robert Kibler and Larry Nichols.

Editorial assistance provided by Cheryl Alcorn, Karen M. Disner, Brenda Koplin, Erica Simmons, and Sharon Young.

Printed in the United States of America by Malloy, Inc.

ISBN 1-884585-63-9

# Contents

*Notes*:

# Introduction to the Third Edition

When students in the social and behavioral sciences take advanced courses in their major field of study, they are often required to read and evaluate original research reports published as articles in academic journals. This book is designed as a guide for students who are first learning how to engage in this process.

## Major Assumptions

First, it is assumed that the students using this book have limited knowledge of research methods, even though they may have taken an introductory research methods course or may be using this book concurrently while taking such a course. Because of this assumption, technical terms and jargon such as "true experiment" are defined and explained when they are first used in this book.

Second, it is assumed that students have only a limited grasp of elementary statistics. Thus, the chapters on evaluating statistical reporting in research reports are confined to criteria such students can handle.

Finally, and perhaps most important, it is assumed that students with limited backgrounds in research methods and statistics can produce adequate evaluations of research reports—evaluations that get to the heart of important issues and allow students to draw sound conclusions from published research.

## This Book is *Not* Written for…

This book is not written for journal editors and members of their editorial review boards. Such professionals usually have had firsthand experience in conducting research and have taken advanced courses in research methods and statistics. Published evaluation criteria for use by these professionals are often terse, filled with jargon, and include many elements that cannot be fully comprehended without advanced training and experience. This book is aimed at a completely different audience: students who are just beginning to learn how to evaluate original reports of research.

## Applying the Evaluation Questions in This Book

Chapters 2 through 13 are organized around evaluation questions that may be answered with a simple "yes" or "no," where a "yes" indicates that you judge a characteristic to be satisfactory. However, for evaluation questions that deal with complex issues, you may also want to rate each one using a scale from 1 to 5, where 5 is the highest rating. N/A (not applicable) may be used if you believe a characteristic does not apply, and I/I (insufficient information) may be used if you believe the research report does not contain sufficient information for you to make an informed judgment.

## Evaluating Quantitative and Qualitative Research

Quantitative and qualitative research differ in purpose as well as methodology. Students who are not familiar with the distinctions between the two approaches are advised to read Appendix A, which presents a very brief overview of the differences, and Appendix B, which provides an overview of important issues in the evaluation of qualitative research. Most research methods textbooks present more detailed accounts of these matters.

## About the Third Edition

Throughout this edition of the book, you will find updated examples that illustrate strengths and weaknesses that you may find in the research you will be evaluating. Also, there is expanded coverage on evaluating Results sections of research reports. In this edition, there are two chapters on this topic: one on evaluating Results sections in *quantitative research* reports (Chapter 10) and one on evaluating Results sections of *qualitative research* reports (Chapter 11).

## Contacting the Author and Publisher

Your comments on this edition as well as suggestions for future editions can be sent to me at Info@Pyrczak.com. You may also write to me at the address provided on the title page of this book. Critical feedback will be welcomed.

My best wishes are with you as you master the art and science of evaluating research. With the aid of this book, I hope that you will find the process not only undaunting but also fascinating as you seek to arrive at defensible conclusions regarding what research indicates about topics of interest to you.

Fred Pyrczak
Los Angeles

# Chapter 1

# Background for Evaluating Research Reports

Academic journals in the social and behavioral sciences abound with original reports of research. These are reports in which researchers describe how they identified a research problem, made relevant observations to gather data, and analyzed the data they collected. The reports usually conclude with a discussion of the results and their implications. This chapter provides an overview of some general characteristics of such research. Subsequent chapters present specific questions that should be applied in the evaluation of research reports.

## ✓ Guideline 1: Researchers very often examine only narrowly defined problems.

*Comment*: While researchers usually are interested in broad problem areas, they very often examine only narrow aspects of the problems due to limited resources and to keep the research manageable by limiting its focus. Furthermore, they often examine them in such a way that the results can be easily reduced to numbers, further limiting their line of vision.[1]

Example 1.1.1 briefly describes a study on whether loneliness leads individuals to engage in self-defeating behavior. To make the study of this issue manageable, the researchers greatly limited its scope. Specifically, they examined only artificially induced "loneliness" and considered only one very narrow type of self-defeating behavior (selecting a lottery with low odds rather than selecting one with high odds).

### Example 1.1.1[2]

*Brief synopsis of a study on the social isolation and loneliness on promoting self-defeating behavior, narrowly defined*:

A sample of college undergraduates was given a personality test. Regardless of how they performed on it, a random half was told that they had the type of per-

---

[1] Qualitative researchers (see Appendices A, B, and D) generally take a broader view in defining a problem to be explored in research and are not constrained by the need to reduce the results to numbers and statistics.

[2] Twenge, J. M., Catanese, K. R., & Baumeister, R. F. (2002). Social exclusion causes self-defeating behavior. *Journal of Personality and Social Psychology, 83*, 606–615.

sonality that would lead them to have few social relationships and be lonely later in life (i.e., the "lonely group"). The other random half was told that their personality profiles indicated that they would have fulfilling social relationships, including long and stable marriages later in life (i.e., the "not lonely group"). These statements were *not* based on the results of the personality test, which was an artificial basis for making the bogus predictions to random groups. Both groups were then given a choice of lotteries in which to participate. One of the lotteries clearly had vastly superior chances of a payoff. The hypothesis was that the "not lonely group" would tend to pick this lottery, while the "lonely group" would tend to pick a lottery with much lower odds of winning. Making the latter choice was taken to be indicative of self-defeating behavior.

Example 1.1.2 is another narrowly focused problem within a broad problem area. Note that the researchers deliberately picked an occupation that is stereotypically held by males. However, it is only one of many such occupations, so the results of the research are limited by the fact that only one occupation is used.

### Example 1.1.2[3]

*Brief synopsis of a study on sexism, narrowly defined*:

Researchers gave three different treatments to see if they could manipulate the expression of sexism among college students. Then they provided a scenario in which the manager of a cement manufacturing company is considering hiring a new employee to obtain new contracts by contacting building contractors and foremen in a highly competitive and harsh market. The students were then asked to rate on a seven-point scale whether a man or a woman would be better suited for the job.

Because researchers often conduct their research on narrowly defined problems, an important task in the evaluation of research is to judge whether a researcher has defined the problem so narrowly that it fails to make an important contribution to the advancement of knowledge. Making this judgment is complicated by the fact that the narrowly defined research of one researcher might contribute to a larger body of knowledge in which the results of a number of narrowly defined studies can be synthesized to reach conclusions that could not reliably be reached based on any individual study.

## ✓ Guideline 2: Researchers often conduct studies in artificial settings.

*Comment*: Artificial settings are usually laboratory settings on university campuses.

---

[3] Monin, B., & Miller, D. T. (2001). Moral credentials and the expression of prejudice. *Journal of Personality and Social Psychology, 81*, 33–43.

To study the effects of alcohol consumption on socialization skills, a group of participants might be asked to drink carefully measured amounts of alcohol in a laboratory while researchers observe their social interactions. To simplify the study so that the results are easily interpreted, the researcher might use a group in which all the members are strangers at the onset of the study. Of course, such a study would have limited generalizability to drinking in out-of-laboratory settings such as nightclubs, at home, at picnics, and other places where those who are consuming alcohol often know each other. Conducting such research in a laboratory, however, allows researchers to simplify and control variables such as the amount of alcohol consumed, what types of people they are interacting with, and so on. Conducting such research in uncontrolled settings such as nightclubs, on the other hand, would lead to results that would be difficult to interpret because there would be many uncontrolled variables (such as the volume of the music or the types and amounts of alcohol consumed) that could interact with the consumption of alcohol in creating the social interaction patterns observed. In short, researchers very often trade off trying to study variables in complex, real-life settings for more interpretable research results that can be obtained in a laboratory.

## ✓ Guideline 3: Researchers use less-than-perfect methods of observation.

*Comment*: In research, *observation* can take many forms—from paper-and-pencil multiple-choice achievement tests to essay examinations, from administering a paper-and-pencil attitude scale with choices from "strongly agree" to "strongly disagree" to conducting unstructured interviews to identify interviewees' attitudes.[4] Of course, *observation* also includes direct observation of people interacting in either their natural environments or laboratory settings.

It is safe to assume that all methods of observation are flawed to some extent. To see why this is so, consider a professor/researcher who is interested in racial relations in society in general. Because of limited resources, the researcher decides to make direct observations of Whites and African Americans interacting (and/or not interacting) in the college cafeteria. The observations will necessarily be limited to the types of behaviors typically exhibited in cafeteria settings—a weakness in the researcher's method of observation. In addition, they will be limited to observations of only certain overt behaviors because it will be difficult for the researcher, for instance, to hear most of what is being said without obtruding on the privacy of the students.

On the other hand, let us suppose that another researcher decides to measure racial attitudes by having students respond anonymously to racial statements by circling "agree" or "disagree" for each one. This researcher has an entirely different set of weaknesses in the observational method. First is the matter of whether students will

---

[4] Researchers usually refer to measurement tools for making observations as *instruments*.

reveal their real attitudes on such a scale—even if the response is anonymous. After all, most college students are aware that negative racial attitudes are severely frowned on in academic communities. Thus, some students might indicate what they believe to be socially desirable (i.e., socially "correct") rather than reveal their true attitudes. In addition, there is the problem of what specific racial statements to include on the scale. For instance, if the statements are too harsh, they might not tap subtle, yet insidious, negative attitudes. Perhaps more important, the statements will be presented in isolation from a real-world context, making it easy for the students to misunderstand the statements or wonder about their full meaning.

We could continue looking at other ways to observe racial attitudes, each time finding potential problems. We could do the same thing for most variables of interest to researchers in the social and behavioral sciences. By now, however, this point is probably clear: There is *no perfect way to measure complex variables*. Instead of expecting perfection, a consumer of research should consider this question: *Is the method sufficiently valid and reliable to provide potentially useful data?*

Frequently, researchers explicitly acknowledge the limitations of their observational methods. Examples 1.3.1 and 1.3.2 show portions of such statements from research articles.

### Example 1.3.1[5]
*Researchers' acknowledgement of limitations of direct observations of behavior*:

Observers did not tape-record actual conversations…but instead relied on their ability to record accurately what they heard. The decision was made not to record conversations verbatim because investigators felt that this might inhibit the natural flow of the conversation…. Second, as with any observational study, the presence of the observer potentially interrupts the "normal" environment, introducing a bias.

### Example 1.3.2[6]
*Researchers' acknowledgment of limitations of self-reports*:

This study is also limited in the fact that the sole data source is a self-report. It is possible that students may respond to the questionnaire in a socially desirable manner and underreport their drinking behaviors.

Chapter 8 provides more information on evaluating observational methods.

---

[5] Solomon, F. M. et al. (2004). Observational study in ten beauty salons: Results informing development of the North Carolina BEAUTY and Health Project. *Health Education & Behavior, 31*, 790–807.
[6] Stamper, G. A., Smith, B. H., Gant, R., & Bogle, K. E. (2004). Replicated findings of an evaluation of a brief intervention designed to prevent high-risk drinking among first-year college students: Implications for social norming theory. *Journal of Alcohol and Drug Education, 48*, 53–72.

## ✓ Guideline 4: Researchers use less-than-perfect samples.

*Comment*: Arguably, the most common sampling flaw in research reported in academic journals is the use of *samples of convenience* (i.e., samples that are readily accessible to the researchers). Most researchers are professors, and professors often use samples of college students—obviously as a matter of convenience. Another common flaw is that of relying on voluntary responses to mailed surveys, which are often quite low, with some researchers arguing that a response rate of about 40% to 60% or more is "acceptable." Other samples are flawed because researchers cannot identify and locate all members of a population (e.g., the homeless). Without being able to do this, it is impossible to draw a sample that a researcher can reasonably defend as being representative of the population.[7] In addition, researchers often have limited resources, forcing them to use small samples, which might produce unreliable results.

Frequently, researchers explicitly acknowledge the limitations of their samples. Examples 1.4.1 through 1.4.3 show portions of such statements from research articles.

### Example 1.4.1[8]

*A researcher's acknowledgment of limitations of sampling (convenience sample at one university)*:

This has been a case study of attrition at a single institution. Thus, this work has been offered as an exploratory study into how attrition occurs at a selective university.... It is unclear whether students from the university used in the present study have any more incentive to leave quietly than do students elsewhere.

### Example 1.4.2[9]

*Researchers' acknowledgment of limitations of sampling (less than perfect response rate to a mailed survey)*:

A questionnaire, cover letter, and business reply envelope were mailed to 1,600 randomly selected registered nurses in Ohio.... As an incentive to return the questionnaires, 50¢ was donated to the American Nurses Foundation for every completed and returned questionnaire.... After 5 weeks and two mailings, a total of 719 (45%) useable surveys were received.

---

[7] Qualitative researchers emphasize selecting a "purposive" sample—one that is likely to yield useful information—rather than a "representative" sample.

[8] Hermanowicz, J. C. (2004). The college departure process among the academic elite. *Education and Urban Society, 37*, 74–93.

[9] Lipson, A. R., Hausman, A. J., Higgins, P. A., & Burant, C. J. (2004). Knowledge, attitudes, and predictors of advance directive discussions of registered nurses. *Western Journal of Nursing Research, 26*, 784–796.

**Example 1.4.3**[10]

*Researchers' acknowledgment of limitations of sampling (small sample size):*

This study had several limitations. First, the small sample size limits the stability of the incidence rates. Unfortunately, recruitment of a larger sample would have required substantially more resources than were available to our research team.

In Chapters 6 and 7, specific criteria for evaluating samples are explored in detail.

## ✓ Guideline 5: Even a seemingly straightforward analysis of data can produce misleading results.

*Comment*: Obviously, data-input errors and computational errors are a possible source of errors in results. Some commercial research firms have the data they collect entered independently by two or more data-entry clerks. A computer program checks to see whether the two sets of entries match perfectly—if not, the errors need to be identified before proceeding with the analysis. Oddly, taking such care in checking for mechanical errors in entering data is hardly ever mentioned in research reports published in academic journals.

In addition, there are alternative statistical methods for most problems, and different methods can yield different results. (See the first evaluation in Chapter 10 for specific examples regarding the selection of statistics.)

Finally, even a nonstatistical analysis can be problematic. For instance, if two or more researchers review extensive transcripts of unstructured interviews, they might differ in their interpretations of the interviewees' responses. Discrepancies such as these suggest that the results may be flawed, or at least subject to different interpretations.

Chapter 10 provides evaluation criteria for quantitative analysis and Results sections of research reports, while Chapter 11 does the same for qualitative analysis and Results sections.

## ✓ Guideline 6: Original reports of research in journals often contain many details, which are of utmost importance when evaluating a report.

*Comment*: The old saying "The devil is in the details" applies here. Students who have relied exclusively on secondary sources for information about their major field of study may be surprised at the level of detail in many research reports, which is typi-

---

[10] Le, H.-N., Muñoz, R. F., Soto, J. A., Delucchi, K. L., & Ippen, C. G. (2004). Identifying risk for onset of major depressive episodes in low-income Latinas during pregnancy and postpartum. *Hispanic Journal of Behavioral Sciences, 26*, 463–482.

cally much greater than even implied in secondary sources such as textbooks and classroom lectures. Example 1.6.1 illustrates the level of detail that you can expect to find in many research reports published in academic journals. It describes part of the procedure used in a study of the important issue of the validity of mug shot identifications in criminal investigations. Note the level of detail such as (1) establishing eye contact with each participant at least two times, (2) having the perpetrator remain in the room approximately 60 seconds, and (3) presenting the mug shots in three photo albums with two 4- by 6-in. (10.16- by 15.24-cm), color, head-and-shoulder pictures on each page. Such details are useful for helping consumers of research picture in their minds exactly what took place in the study. They are also helpful for other researchers who might want to replicate the study to see if they can confirm the findings.

### Example 1.6.1[11]

*An excerpt from an article illustrating the level of detail often reported in research reports in academic journals:*

A female experimenter met 1 to 3 participants at the door of the laboratory and led them into a small room. After seating the participants, the experimenter told them that she had to leave the room to get some forms. She then removed a set of keys from her purse and placed the purse on a nearby table. As the experimenter was leaving the room, a male confederate (the perpetrator) knocked on the door and asked if he was at the right location for the psychology experiment. After being told that he was, he was asked to enter the room and wait for the experimenter to return. The confederate then entered the room and engaged the participants in conversation (e.g., "Did she say how long she was going to be gone?") until he established eye contact twice with each participant. At that point, he grabbed the experimenter's purse and fled the room. The perpetrator was present in the room for approximately 60 seconds.

  Immediately after the perpetrator exited, the experimenter returned and informed the participants that they had witnessed a staged crime. Participants were informed of the nature of the experiment and asked to sign a consent form. Then, participants gave a written description of the perpetrator and made arrangements to return the following day. Participants who had been randomly assigned to the no-mug-shot conditions ($n = 52$) were dismissed after completing the description of the criminal and scheduling a return time for the next day. Those who had been randomly assigned to the mug-shot conditions ($n = 52$) viewed mug shots for the remainder of the 30-min session or until they had seen 600 mug shots. The total number of mug shots viewed was determined by how long the participants had taken to complete the description of the perpetrator and their (self-determined) pace of examining the mug shots. Participants were asked to record the picture numbers of any mug shots that they thought were or may have been of the perpetrator. The mug shots were presented in three photo albums with two 4- by 6-in. (10.16- by 15.24-cm), color, head-and-shoulder pictures on each page. Neither the perpetrator's photograph nor any of the lineup members appeared in the mug-shot albums.

  Having detailed information on what was said to and done to participants as well as on how the participants were observed makes it possible to make informed evaluations of research.

---

[11] Dysart, J. E., Lindsay, R. C. L., Hammond, R., & Dupuis, P. (2001). Mug shot exposure prior to lineup identification: Interference, transference, and commitment effects. *Journal of Applied Psychology, 86,* 1280–1284.

✓ **Guideline 7: Even highly detailed reports often lack information on matters that are potentially important for evaluating a research article.**

*Comment*: When you begin reading journal articles, you may be surprised to find that even major studies on very important issues are covered in rather brief reports. In most journals, research reports of more than about 15 pages are rare. Journal space is limited by economics—journals have limited readership and thus a limited paid circulation, and they seldom have advertisers. Given this situation, researchers must judiciously choose the details they will report. Sometimes, they may omit information that readers deem important.

Omitted details can cause problems when evaluating research. For example, it is common for researchers to describe in general terms the questionnaires and attitude scales they used without reporting the exact wording of the questions.[12] Yet, there is considerable research indicating that how items are worded can affect the results of a study. Of course, judgments about the adequacy of the items cannot be made in their absence.

As you apply the evaluation questions throughout this book while evaluating research, you may be surprised at how often you must answer "insufficient information to make a judgment." If this is your response to many of the questions for a given research report, you may well conclude that the report is too lacking in details to make an important contribution to the knowledge base on the topic of the research.

✓ **Guideline 8: Some published research reports are methodologically very weak.**

*Comment*: With many hundreds of editors of and contributors to academic journals, it is understandable that published research reports vary in quality, with some being very weak in terms of their research methodology.[13]

Undoubtedly, some weak reports simply slip past less-skilled editors. More likely, an editor may make a deliberate decision to publish a weak report because the problem it explores is of current interest to his or her readers. Consider one example to illustrate the justification for such a decision: the issue of charter schools, which is

---

[12] This statement appears in each issue of *The Gallup Poll Monthly*: "In addition to sampling error, readers should bear in mind that question wording…can introduce additional systematic error or 'bias' into the results of opinion polls." Accordingly, *The Gallup Poll Monthly* reports the exact wording of the questions they use in their polls. Other researchers cannot always do this because the measures they use may be too long to include in the report or may be copyrighted by publishers who do not want the items released to the public.

[13] Many journals are "refereed." This means that the editor has experts act as referees by evaluating each paper submitted for possible publication. These experts make their judgments without knowing the identification of the researcher who submitted the paper, and the editor uses their input in deciding which papers to publish as journal articles.

currently a topic of great interest in education. Briefly, a charter school is one that is allowed to bypass many of the government dictates on how schools must operate, giving parents, teachers, and principals freedom to collaborate in order to establish processes that may deviate from the norm, presumably in the best interests of the students. Let us suppose that a researcher wants to compare the progress of students enrolled in charter schools with those in schools that do not have charter status. He or she has a methodological problem. Specifically, students are not assigned to schools at random (like drawing names out of a hat). Therefore, the students in the two types of schools may initially differ substantially in terms of a number of characteristics that may affect their educational progress, such as their socioeconomic backgrounds, their parents' involvement in the schools, their motivation to learn, and so on. In other words, differences in students' progress between the two types of schools might be the result of (a) initial differences between the two groups of students or (b) differences in the programs they receive (charter vs. noncharter programs).[14] The editor of an education journal might reasonably conclude that publishing studies with this weakness is better than publishing no studies on this important and increasingly widespread educational reform.

Sometimes, studies with very serious methodological problems are labeled as *pilot studies*, either in their titles or introductions to the research reports. A pilot study is a preliminary study that allows a researcher to try out new methods and procedures for conducting research, often with small samples. Pilot studies may be refined in subsequent, more definitive studies. Publication of pilot studies, despite their limited samples and other potential weaknesses, is justified on the basis that they may point other researchers in the direction of promising new leads for further research.

## ✓ Guideline 9: No research report provides "proof."

*Comment*: Conducting research is fraught with pitfalls, and any one study may have very misleading results. This is not to suggest, however, that research should be abandoned as a method for advancing knowledge. Instead, the solution is, in part, to evaluate individual research reports carefully to identify those that are most likely to provide sound results. The second part of the solution is to look across studies on the same research problem. If different researchers using different research methods with different types of strengths and weaknesses all reach similar conclusions, we can say that we have *considerable confidence* in the conclusions of the body of research. On the other hand, to the extent that the body of research on a topic yields mixed results, we will lower our degree of confidence. For instance, if the studies that we judge indi-

---

[14] Statistical methods may be used to take account of initial differences between students in the two types of schools, but these methods depend on the ability to identify and validly measure all the important differences that may affect the outcomes of the study. Even if a researcher makes a strong argument that this has been done in a particular study, the outcome is far less satisfactory than what would be obtained by assigning students at random to the two types of schools.

vidually to be strong all point in the same direction while weaker ones point in a different direction, we might say that we have *some confidence* in the conclusion suggested by the stronger studies.

A caveat: If an individual states that "research *proves* that X is related to Z," you will know that you are receiving information from a naïve person, which should cause you to beware. Another statement that is a sign of a naïve or careless individual is "this study *shows* that X is related to Z." Listeners are likely to infer from such a statement that "shows" means "proves" and that a single study can prove something. Professionals who have studied and carefully considered research methods and statistics will hedge their remarks, using statements such as "this study *suggests* that…," "an important study *provides strong evidence* that…," or "a pilot study provides *preliminary information indicating* that…."

## ✓ Guideline 10: Other things being equal, research related to theories is more important than nontheoretical research.

A given theory helps explain interrelationships among a number of variables and often has implications for understanding human behavior in a variety of settings. Studies that have results consistent with a theory lend support to the theory. Those with inconsistent results argue against the theory. After a number of studies relating to the theory have been conducted, their results provide accumulated evidence that argues for or against the theory as well as evidence that can assist in modifying the theory. Often, researchers explicitly discuss theories that are relevant to their research, as illustrated in Example 1.10.1.

### Example 1.10.1[15]

*Portions of researchers' discussion of a theory related to their research*:

One of the most influential theories regarding women's intentions to stay in or leave abusive relationships is social exchange theory, which suggests that these kinds of relational decisions follow from an analysis of the relative cost-benefit ratio of remaining in a relationship (Kelley & Thibaut, 1978). On the basis of this theory, many researchers have posited that whereas escaping the abuse may appear to be a clear benefit, the costs associated with leaving the relationship may create insurmountable barriers for many abused women.

The role of theoretical considerations in the evaluation of research is discussed in greater detail in Chapter 4.

---

[15] Gordon, K. C., Burton, S., & Porter, L. (2004). Predicting the intentions of women in domestic violence shelters to return to partners: Does forgiveness play a role? *Journal of Family Psychology, 18*, 331–338.

## ✓ Guideline 11: To become an expert on a topic, you must become an expert at evaluating original reports of research.

*Comment*: An expert is someone who knows not only broad generalizations about a topic but also the nuances of the research that underlie them; that is, he or she knows the particular strengths and weaknesses of the major studies used to arrive at the generalizations. For instance, suppose a school board hires an expert on reading instruction to assist with a decision regarding the emphasis to place on phonics and whole language methods of reading instruction.[16] Members of the board should expect the expert to be familiar with the range of research on this controversy as well as the quality of individual studies on the topic. Such an expert should be able to make recommendations based on generalizations reached by considering the *quality of the evidence* found in research reports. He or she should be able to point out what is likely to be true and untrue based on careful evaluations of relevant research.

As you begin taking upper-division courses, your goal should be to become an expert on the topics central to the profession for which you are preparing, and you can do this only by carefully evaluating the research on these topics. At the graduate level, you will not only want to refine your expertise but also make creative contributions by conducting new research. Careful and insightful review and evaluation of existing research will help you become a better researcher because you will learn from the mistakes and triumphs of other researchers. Immersing yourself in and evaluating published research, much of which is highly creative, is likely to spark your own creative abilities.

# Exercise for Chapter 1

**Part A**

*Directions*: The 11 guidelines discussed in this chapter are repeated below. For each one, indicate the extent to which you were already familiar with it before reading this chapter. Use a scale from 1 (not at all familiar) to 5 (very familiar).

**Guideline 1**: Researchers very often examine only narrowly defined problems.

Familiarity rating:   5    4    3    2    1

---

[16] As you may know, phonics stresses sounding out letters and parts of words. Whole language emphasizes providing a rich language environment (e.g., many complete books, numerous verbal experiences such as reading books to students) that stimulates children to learn to read.

**Guideline 2**: Researchers often conduct studies in artificial settings.

Familiarity rating:   5   4   3   2   1

**Guideline 3**: Researchers use less-than-perfect methods of observation.

Familiarity rating:   5   4   3   2   1

**Guideline 4**: Researchers use less-than-perfect samples.

Familiarity rating:   5   4   3   2   1

**Guideline 5**: Even a seemingly straightforward analysis of data can produce misleading results.

Familiarity rating:   5   4   3   2   1

**Guideline 6**: Original reports of research in journals often contain many details, which are of utmost importance when evaluating a report.

Familiarity rating:   5   4   3   2   1

**Guideline 7**: Even highly detailed reports often lack information on matters that are potentially important for evaluating a research article.

Familiarity rating:   5   4   3   2   1

**Guideline 8**: Some published research reports are methodologically very weak.

Familiarity rating:   5   4   3   2   1

**Guideline 9**: No research report provides "proof."

Familiarity rating:   5   4   3   2   1

**Guideline 10**: Other things being equal, research related to theories is more important than nontheoretical research.

Familiarity rating:   5   4   3   2   1

**Guideline 11**: To become an expert on a topic, you must become an expert at evaluating original reports of research.

Familiarity rating:   5   4   3   2   1

**Part B:  Application**

*Directions*: Read a report of research published in an academic journal and respond to the following questions. The report may be one that you select or one that is assigned by your instructor. If you are using this book without any prior training in research methods, do the best you can in answering the questions at this point. As you work through this book, your evaluations will become increasingly sophisticated.

1. How narrowly is the research problem defined? In your opinion, is it too narrow? Is it too broad? Explain.

2. Was the research setting artificial (e.g., a laboratory setting)? If yes, do you think that the gain in the control of extraneous variables offsets the potential loss of information that would be obtained in a study in a more real-life setting? Explain.

3. Are there any obvious flaws or weaknesses in the researcher's methods of observation? Explain. (Note: Observation or measurement is often described under the subheading "Instrumentation.")

4. Are there any obvious sampling flaws? Explain.

5. Was the analysis statistical or nonstatistical? Was the description of the results easy to understand? Explain.

6. Were the descriptions of procedures and methods of observation sufficiently detailed? Were any important details missing? Explain.

7. Does the report lack information on matters that are potentially important for evaluating it?

8. Overall, was the research obviously very weak? If yes, briefly describe its weaknesses and speculate on why it was published despite them.

9. Does the researcher describe related theories?

10. Does the researcher imply that his or her research *proves* something? Do you believe that it proves something? Explain.

11. Do you think that as a result of reading this chapter and evaluating a research report that you are becoming more expert at evaluating research reports? Explain.

*Notes*:

# Chapter 2

# Evaluating Titles

The primary function of titles is to help consumers of research identify journal articles of interest to them. A preliminary evaluation of a title should be made when it is first encountered. After the article is read, the title should be reevaluated to ensure that it accurately reflects the contents of the article.

Apply the evaluation questions while you evaluate a research article. The questions are stated as "yes–no" questions, where a "yes" indicates that you judge the characteristic to be satisfactory. You may also want to rate each characteristic using a scale from 1 to 5, where 5 is the highest rating. N/A (not applicable) and I/I (insufficient information to make a judgment) may also be used when necessary.

## ____ 1. Is the title sufficiently specific?

Very satisfactory  5  4  3  2  1  Very unsatisfactory  *or*  N/A  I/I

*Comment*: On any major topic in the social and behavioral sciences, there are likely to be many hundreds of research reports published in academic journals. In order to help potential readers locate those that are most relevant to their needs, researchers should use titles that are sufficiently specific so that each article can be differentiated from the other research articles on the same topic.

Consider the topic of depression, which has been very extensively investigated. The title in Example 2.1.1 is insufficiently specific. Contrast it with the titles in Example 2.1.2, which contain information that differentiates each article from the others.

### Example 2.1.1
*A title that is insufficiently specific:*

An Investigation of Adolescent Depression and Its Implications

### Example 2.1.2
*Three titles that are more specific than the one in Example 2.1.1:*

Gender Differences in the Expression of Depression by Early Adolescent Children of Alcoholics

The Impact of Social Support on the Severity of Postpartum Depression Among Adolescent Mothers

The Effectiveness of Cognitive Therapy in the Treatment of Adolescent Students with Severe Clinical Depression

## ___ 2. Is the title reasonably concise?

Very satisfactory 5 4 3 2 1 Very unsatisfactory *or* N/A I/I

*Comment*: While a title should be specific (see the previous evaluation question), it should be fairly concise. Titles of research articles in academic journals typically are about 15 words or less. When a title contains more than 20 words, it is likely that the researcher is providing more information than is needed by consumers of research in order to locate research articles of interest.[1]

## ___ 3. Are the primary variables referred to in the title?

Very satisfactory 5 4 3 2 1 Very unsatisfactory *or* N/A I/I

*Comment*: Variables are the characteristics of the participants that varied from one participant to another. In Example 2.3.1, the variables are the (1) television viewing habits, (2) mathematics achievement, and (3) reading achievement. For instance, the children could *vary* (or differ) in their reading achievement, with some children achieving more than others. Likewise, they could vary in terms of their mathematics achievement and their television viewing habits.

### Example 2.3.1
*A title that mentions three variables*:

The Relationship Between Young Children's Television Viewing Habits and Their Achievement in Mathematics and Reading

Note that "young children" is *not* a variable because the title clearly suggests that only young children were studied. In other words, being a young child is a *common trait* of all the participants. (The matter of identifying traits that are common to a population in a title is discussed under the next evaluation question.)

When researchers examine many specific variables in a given study, they appropriately may refer to the *types* of variables in their titles rather than naming each one individually. For instance, suppose a researcher administered a major achievement test that measured spelling ability, reading comprehension, vocabulary knowledge, mathematical problem-solving skills, and so on. Naming all these variables would create a title that is much too long (see the previous evaluation question). Instead, the researcher could refer to this collection of variables measured by the test as *academic achievement*, which is done in Example 2.3.2.

---

[1] Titles of theses and dissertations tend to be longer than those of journal articles.

**Example 2.3.2**

*A title in which types of variables (achievement variables) are identified without naming the specific achievement variables*:

The Relationship Between Parental Involvement in Schooling and Academic Achievement in the Middle Grades

## ___ 4. Does the title identify the types of individuals who participated?

Very satisfactory  5  4  3  2  1  Very unsatisfactory  *or*  N/A  I/I

*Comment*: Research methods textbooks suggest that researchers should name the population(s) of interest in their research reports. It follows that it is often desirable to include names of populations in the titles. From the title in Example 2.4.1, it would be reasonable to infer that the population of interest consists of graduate students who are taking a statistics class. This would be of interest to a consumer of research who is searching through a list of the many hundreds of articles that have been published on cooperative learning. Knowing that the report deals with this particular population might help a consumer rule it out as an article if, for instance, he or she is trying to locate research on the use of cooperative learning in teaching elementary school mathematics.

**Example 2.4.1**

*A title in which the type of participants is mentioned*:

Effects of Cooperative Learning in a Graduate-Level Statistics Class

Example 2.4.2 also names an important characteristic of the research participants—the fact that they are registered nurses employed by hospitals.

**Example 2.4.2**

*A title in which the type of participants is mentioned*:

Administrative Management Styles and Job Satisfaction Among Registered Nurses Employed by Public Hospitals

Often, researchers use participants only because they are readily available, such as college students enrolled in an introductory psychology class who are required to participate in research projects. Researchers might use such individuals even though they are conducting research that might apply to all types of individuals. For instance, a researcher might conduct research to test a social relations theory that might apply to all types of individuals. In such a case, the researcher might omit mentioning the types of individuals (e.g., college students) in the title because the research is not specifically directed at that population.

## ____ 5. If a study is strongly tied to a theory, is the name of the specific theory mentioned in the title?

Very satisfactory  5  4  3  2  1  Very unsatisfactory  *or*  N/A  I/I

*Comment*: Theories help to advance science because they are propositions regarding relationships that have applications in many diverse specific situations. For instance, a particular learning theory might have applications for teaching kindergarten children as well as for training astronauts. A useful theory leads to predictions about human behavior that can be tested through research. Many consumers of research are seeking information on specific theories, and mention of them in titles helps these consumers identify reports of relevant research. On the other hand, if the research has a theoretical basis but the research is not specifically designed to test the theory, reference to the theory might instead be made in the abstract, which will be considered in the next chapter. Example 2.5.1 shows two titles in which specific theories are mentioned.

### Example 2.5.1[2,3]
*Two titles that mention specific theories (desirable)*:

Application of Adult Attachment Theory to Treatment of Chronically Suicidal, Traumatized Women

The Importance of Being Nonalignable: A Critical Test of the Structural Alignment Theory of Similarity

Note that simply using the term "theory" in a title without mentioning the name of the specific theory is not useful to consumers of research. Example 2.5.2 has this undesirable characteristic.

### Example 2.5.2
*A title that refers to theory without naming the specific theory (undesirable)*:

An Examination of Voting Patterns and Social Class in a Rural Southern Community: A Study Based on Theory

## ____ 6. Does the title indicate the nature of the research without describing the results?

Very satisfactory  5  4  3  2  1  Very unsatisfactory  *or*  N/A  I/I

*Comment*: It is usually inappropriate for a title to describe the results of a research project. Use of observational methods, which are inherently flawed as noted in Chapter 1,

---

[2] Gormley, B. (2004). *Psychotherapy: Theory, Research, Practice, Training, 41*, 136–143.
[3] Estes, Z., & Hasson, U. (2004). *Journal of Experimental Psychology: Learning, Memory, & Cognition, 30*, 1082–1092.

often raise more questions than answers. In addition, the research results often can be subject to more than one interpretation. Consider the title in Example 2.6.1, which undoubtedly oversimplifies the results of the study. An accounting of the results should address issues such as: What type of social support (e.g., parental support, peer support, and so on) is effective? How strong does it need to be to lessen the depression? By how much is depression lessened by strong social support? and so on. Because it is usually impossible to state results accurately and unambiguously in a short title, results ordinarily should *not* be stated at all, as illustrated in Example 2.6.2.

### Example 2.6.1

*A title that inappropriately describes results*:

Strong Social Support Lessens Depression in Delinquent Young Adolescents

### Example 2.6.2

*A title that appropriately does not describe results*:

The Relationship Between Social Support and Depression in Delinquent Young Adolescents

## ___ 7. Has the author avoided using a "yes–no" question as a title?

Very satisfactory  5  4  3  2  1  Very unsatisfactory  *or*  N/A  I/I

*Comment*: Because research rarely yields simple, definitive answers, it is seldom appropriate to use a title that poses a simple "yes–no" question. For instance, Example 2.7.1 implies that there is a simple answer to the question it poses. However, a study on this topic undoubtedly explores *the extent to which men and women differ in their opinions on social justice issues*—a much more interesting topic than suggested by the title. Example 2.7.2 is cast as a statement and is more appropriate as the title of a research report for publication in an academic journal.

### Example 2.7.1

*A title that inappropriately poses a "yes–no" question*:

Do Men and Women Differ in Their Opinions on Social Justice Issues?

### Example 2.7.2

*A more appropriate title than the one in Example 2.7.1*:

Gender Differences in Opinions on Social Justice Issues

**___ 8. If there is a main title and a subtitle, do both provide important information about the research?**

Very satisfactory   5   4   3   2   1   Very unsatisfactory   *or*   N/A   I/I

*Comment*: Failure on this evaluation question often results from an author using a "clever" main title that is vague, followed by a subtitle that identifies the specific content of the research report. Example 2.8.1 illustrates this problem. As you can see, the main title is vague and fails to impart specific information. In fact, it could apply to many thousands of studies in hundreds of fields as diverse as psychology and physics in which researchers find that various combinations of variables (the parts) contribute to our understanding of a complex whole.

### Example 2.8.1
*A two-part title with a vague main title*:

The Whole Is Greater Than the Sum of Its Parts: The Relationship Between Playing with Pets and Longevity Among the Elderly

Example 2.8.2 is also deficient because the main title is vague.

### Example 2.8.2
*A two-part title with a vague main title*:

The Other Side of the Story: The Relationship Between Social Class and Mothers' Involvement in Their Children's Schooling

In contrast to the above two examples, Example 2.8.3 has a main title and a subtitle, both of which refer to specific variables examined in a research study. The first part names two major variables ("attachment" and "well-being") while the second part names the two groups that were compared in terms of these variables.

### Example 2.8.3
*A two-part title in which both parts provide important information*:

Attachment to Parents and Emotional Well-Being: A Comparison of African American and White Adolescents

The title in Example 2.8.3 could be rewritten as a single statement without a subtitle, as illustrated in Example 2.8.4.

### Example 2.8.4
*A rewritten version of Example 2.8.3*:

A Comparison of the Emotional Well-Being and Attachment to Parents of African American and White Adolescents

Do you think that Example 2.8.3 or 2.8.4 is a more effective and efficient title? The answer is arguable. Thus, the evaluation question we are considering here is neutral on whether a title should be broken into a main title and subtitle. Rather, it suggests that if it is broken into two parts, both parts should provide important information specific to the research being reported.

## ___ 9. If the title implies causality, does the method of research justify it?

Very satisfactory   5   4   3   2   1   Very unsatisfactory   *or*   N/A   I/I

*Comment*: Example 2.9.1 implies that causal relationships have been examined because it contains the word *effects*. In fact, this is a keyword frequently used by researchers in their titles to indicate that they have explored causality in their studies. A common method to examine causal relationships is to conduct an *experiment*. As you may know, an experiment is a study in which different groups of participants are given different treatments (such as giving one group computer-assisted instruction while using a more traditional method to teach another group). The researcher compares the outcomes obtained by applying the various treatments.[4] When such a study is conducted, the use of the word "effects" in the title is justified.[5]

### Example 2.9.1
*A title in which causality is implied by the word "effects"*:

The Effects of Computer-Assisted Instruction in Mathematics on Students' Achievements and Attitudes

The title in Example 2.9.2 also suggests that the researcher examined a causal relationship because of the inclusion of the word *effects*. Note that in this case, however, the researcher probably did *not* investigate the relationship using an experiment because it would be unethical/illegal to manipulate breakfast as an independent variable (i.e., researchers would not want to assign some students to receive breakfast while denying it to others for the purposes of an experiment).

---

[4] Experiments can also be conducted by treating a given person or group differently *at different points in time*. For example, we might praise a child for staying in his or her seat in the classroom on some days and not praise him or her on others while comparing the child's seat-staying behavior under the two conditions.
[5] The evaluation of experiments is considered in Chapter 9. Note that this evaluation question merely asks if there is a basis for suggesting causality in the title (i.e., reference to causality may be justified even if the research methods are subject to criticism as long as the author attempted to use methods appropriate for examining causality). This evaluation question does not ask you to judge the quality of the experiment or ex post facto study.

**Example 2.9.2**

*A title in which causality is implied by the word "effects":*

The Effects of Breakfast on Student Achievement in the Primary Grades

When it is not possible to conduct an experiment on a causal issue, researchers often conduct what are called *ex post facto* (i.e., *causal–comparative*) studies. In these studies, researchers identify students who are different on some outcome (such as students who are high and low in achievement in the primary grades) but who are the same on demographics and other potentially influential variables (such as parents' highest level of education, parental income, quality of the schools the children attend, and so on). Comparing the breakfast eating habits of the two groups (i.e., high and low achievement groups) might yield some useful information on whether eating breakfast *affects*[6] students' achievement because the two groups are similar on other variables that might account for differences in achievement (e.g., their parents' level of education is similar). If a researcher has conducted such a study, the use of the word *effects* in the title is justified.

Note that simply examining a relationship without controlling for potentially confounding variables does *not* justify a reference to causality in the title. For example, if a researcher merely compared the achievement of children who regularly eat breakfast with those who do not without controlling for other explanatory variables, a causal conclusion (and, hence, a title suggesting it) usually cannot be justified.

Also note that synonyms for *effect* are *influence* and *impact*. They should usually be reserved for use in titles of studies that are either experiments or ex post facto studies.

## ___ 10. Is the title free of jargon and acronyms that might be unknown to the audience for the research report?

Very satisfactory   5   4   3   2   1   Very unsatisfactory   *or*   N/A   I/I

*Comment*: Professionals in all fields use jargon and acronyms (i.e., shorthand for words and usually spelled in all capital letters) for efficient and accurate communication with their peers. However, their use in titles of research reports is inappropriate unless the researchers are writing exclusively for such peers. Consider Example 2.10.1. If ACOA is likely to be well-known to all the readers of the journal in which this title appeared, its use is probably appropriate; otherwise, it should be spelled out or its meaning paraphrased. As you can see, it is difficult to make this judgment without being familiar with the journal and its audience. Nevertheless, if you are reading an article on a topic on which you have already read extensively and encounter an ac-

---

[6] Note that when referring to an outcome caused by some agent, the word is spelled *effects* (i.e., it is a noun). As a verb meaning "to influence," the word is spelled *affects*.

ronym that you do not understand in the title of an article, its use is probably inappropriate.[7]

**Example 2.10.1**
*A title with an acronym that is not spelled out (may be inappropriate if not well–known by the audience of readers)*:

Job Satisfaction and Motivation to Succeed Among ACOA in Managerial Positions

___ **11. Overall, is the title effective and appropriate?**

Very satisfactory  5  4  3  2  1  Very unsatisfactory  *or*  N/A  I/I

*Comment*: Rate this evaluation question after considering your answers to the earlier ones in this chapter and any additional considerations and concerns you may have after reading the entire research article. Be prepared to rewrite the titles of research reports to which you assign low ratings.

# Exercise for Chapter 2

**Part A**

*Directions*: Evaluate each of the following titles to the extent that it is possible to do so without reading the complete research reports. The references for the titles are given below; all are from journals that are widely available in large academic libraries, making it possible for you to consult the complete articles if they are assigned by your instructor. More definitive application of the evaluation criteria for titles is possible by reading the complete articles and then evaluating their titles. Keep in mind that there can be considerable subjectivity in determining whether a title is adequate.

1. Impact of the Special Supplemental Nutrition Program for Women, Infants, and Children on the Healthy Eating Behaviors of Preschool Children in Eastern Idaho[8]

2. Being a Sibling[9]

3. Parent-Child Relations and Children's Psychological Well-Being: Do Dads Matter?[10]

---

[7] As you may know, ACOA stands for Adult Children of Alcoholics.
[8] Dundas, M. L., & Cook, K. (2004). *Topics in Clinical Nutrition, 19*, 273–279.
[9] Baumann, S. L., Dyches, T. T., & Braddick, M. (2005). *Nursing Science Quarterly, 18*, 51–58.
[10] Videon, T. M. (2005). *Journal of Family Issues, 26*, 55–78.

4. Beating the Odds: Teaching Middle and High School Students to Read and Write Well[11]

5. Aggressive Adolescents Benefit from Massage Therapy[12]

6. The Third Eye[13]

7. Students Prefer the Immediate Feedback Assessment Technique[14]

8. Designing Emotionally Sound Instruction: An Empirical Validation of the FEASP Approach[15]

9. Does Funding for HIV and Sexually Transmitted Disease Prevention Matter?[16]

10. Police Lineups: Data, Theory, and Policy[17]

11. Is Cleanliness Next to Godliness? The Role of Housekeeping in Impression Formation[18]

**Part B**

*Directions*: Examine several academic journals that publish on topics of interest to you. Identify two with titles you think are especially strong in terms of the evaluation questions presented in this chapter. Also, identify two titles that clearly have weaknesses. Bring the four titles to class for discussion.

---

[11] Langer, J. A. (2001). *American Educational Research Journal, 38,* 837.
[12] Diego, M. A. et al. (2002). *Adolescence, 37,* 597.
[13] Eken, A. N. (2002). *Journal of Adolescent & Adult Literacy, 46,* 220.
[14] Epstein, M. L., & Brosvic, G. M. (2002). *Psychological Reports, 90,* 1136.
[15] Astleitner, H. (2001). *Journal of Instructional Psychology, 28,* 209.
[16] Chesson, H. W., Harrison, P., Scotton, C. R., & Varghese, B. (2005). *Evaluation Review, 29,* 3–23.
[17] Wells, G. L. (2001). *Psychology, Public Policy, and Law, 7,* 791.
[18] Harris, P. B., & Sachau, D. (2005). *Environment and Behavior, 37,* 81–101.

# Chapter 3

# Evaluating Abstracts

An abstract is a summary of a research report that appears below its title. Like the title, it helps consumers of research identify articles of interest. This function of abstracts is so important that the major computerized databases in the social and behavioral sciences provide abstracts as well as the titles of the articles they index.

Many journals have a policy on the maximum length of abstracts. It is common to allow a maximum of about 100 to 250 words.[1] When evaluating abstracts, you will need to make subjective decisions about how much weight should be given to the various elements that might be included, given that their length typically is severely restricted.

Make a preliminary evaluation of an abstract when you first encounter it. After reading the associated article, reevaluate the abstract. The evaluation questions below are stated as "yes–no" questions, where a "yes" indicates that you judge the characteristic being considered as satisfactory. You may also want to rate each characteristic using a scale from 1 to 5, where 5 is the highest rating. N/A (not applicable) and I/I (insufficient information to make a judgment) may also be used when necessary.

## ____ 1. Is the purpose of the study referred to or at least clearly implied?

Very satisfactory  5  4  3  2  1  Very unsatisfactory  *or*  N/A  I/I

*Comment*: Many writers begin their abstracts with a brief statement of the purpose of their research. Examples 3.1.1 and 3.1.2 show the first sentences of abstracts in which this was done. Note that even though the word "purpose" is not used in Example 3.1.2, the purpose is clearly implied.

### Example 3.1.1[2]
*First sentence of an abstract that specifically states the purpose of the study (acceptable)*:

The purpose of this study is to investigate differences in attitudes toward rape between Asian and Caucasian college students.

---

[1] The *Publication Manual of the American Psychological Association* suggests that an abstract should not exceed 120 words.
[2] Lee, J., Pomeroy, E. C., Yoo, S.-K., & Rheinboldt, K. T. (2005). Attitudes toward rape: A comparison between Asian and Caucasian College Students. *Violence Against Women, 11*, 177–196.

**Example 3.1.2**[3]

*First sentence of an abstract that implies the purpose of the study (also acceptable)*:

The study explores cultural influences on depression and care outcomes among Asian Indians with depression.

Beginning an abstract with an explicit statement of the research purpose is not necessary if the purpose can be inferred from the title and other information contained in the abstract. Consider the title and beginning of the abstract shown in Example 3.1.3. Taken in their entirety, the title and the abstract together make it easy to infer that the purpose is to explore how children acquire work-related values and expectations through dinnertime conversations with working parents.

**Example 3.1.3**[4]

*A title and complete abstract that clearly imply the purpose of the study*:

*Title of an article*: Learning About Work at Dinnertime: Language Socialization in Dual-Earner American Families

*The associated abstract*: The relation between work and family is a topic of considerable research and analysis across disciplines. Yet, few studies have examined how children are socialized into working family life through routine social interactions with family members. This study integrates the lives of children more fully into the literature through a language socialization approach. It analyzes video-recorded dinnertime conversations among 16 middle-class working families in Los Angeles to illuminate how children are apprenticed into discourses and ideologies of work. Children acquire work-related values and expectations, as well as related narrative and analytical skills, through taking part in and overhearing their parents' conversations about work.

## ____ 2. Does the abstract highlight the research methodology?

Very satisfactory  5  4  3  2  1  Very unsatisfactory  *or*  N/A  I/I

*Comment*: Given the shortness of an abstract, researchers usually can provide only limited details on their research methodology. However, even brief highlights can be helpful to consumers of research who are searching for research reports of interest. Consider Example 3.2.1, which is taken from an abstract. The fact that the research participants were randomly assigned to treatment and control conditions and that ef-

---

[3] Conrad, M. M., & Pacquiao, D. F. (2005). Manifestation, attribution, and coping with depression among Asian Indians from the perspectives of health care practitioners. *Journal of Transcultural Nursing*, *16*, 32–40.
[4] Paugh, A. L. (2005). Learning about work at dinnertime: Language socialization in dual-earner American families. *Discourse and Society*, *16*, 55–78.

fects were examined over a long time period (i.e., 3 years) are important methodological strengths that might set this study apart from others on the same topic.[5]

**Example 3.2.1**[6]
*Excerpt from an abstract that describes highlights of research methodology (desirable)*:

This study reports results from interviews with 157 research participants who were interviewed 3 years after randomization into treatment and control conditions in the evaluation of the Baltimore City Drug Treatment Court. The interviews asked about crime, substance use, welfare, employment, education, mental and physical health, and family and social relationships.

Likewise, the information in Example 3.2.2 provides important information about the researchers' research methodology: the fact that a nationwide sample was used.

**Example 3.2.2**[7]
*Excerpt from an abstract that describes highlights of research methodology (desirable)*:

Interviews were conducted with a nationwide sample of older adults at three points in time. Survey items were administered to assess exposure to negative interaction [i.e., interpersonal conflict], socioeconomic status, and whether study participants had heart disease.

## ___ 3. Has the researcher omitted the titles of measures (except when these are the focus of the research)?

Very satisfactory  5  4  3  2  1  Very unsatisfactory  *or*  N/A  I/I

*Comment*: Including the full, formal titles of published measures such as tests, questionnaires, and scales in an abstract is *usually* inappropriate (see the exception below) because their names take up space that could be used to convey more important information.[8] Note that consumers of research who are interested in the topic will be able to find the full names of the instruments in the body of the research report, where space is less limited than in an abstract. A comparison of Examples 3.3.1 and 3.3.2 shows

---

[5] Studies in which participants are randomly assigned to treatment conditions are known as *true experiments*.
[6] Gottfredson, D. C., Kearley, B. W., Najaka, S. S., & Rocha, C. M. (2005). The Baltimore City Drug Treatment Court: 3-year self-reported outcome study. *Evaluation Review, 29*, 42–64.
[7] Krause, N. (2005). Negative interaction and heart disease in late life: Exploring variations by socioeconomic status. *Journal of Aging and Health, 17*, 28–55.
[8] Note that in many of the social and behavioral sciences, the generic terms "instrument" and "instrumentation" are often used to refer to measures such as tests, scales, interview questions, etc.

how much space can be saved by omitting the names of the instruments, while conveying the same essential information.

### Example 3.3.1
*An excerpt from an abstract that names the titles of measures (inappropriate due to space limitations in abstracts)*:

A sample of 483 college males completed the Attitudes Toward Alcohol Scale (Fourth Edition, Revised), the Alcohol Use Questionnaire, and the Manns-Herschfield Quantitative Inventory of Alcohol Dependence (Brief Form).

### Example 3.3.2
*An improved version of Example 3.3.1*:

A sample of 483 college males completed measures of their attitudes toward alcohol, their alcohol use, and their dependence on alcohol.

*The exception*: If the primary purpose of the research is to evaluate the reliability and validity of one or more specific measures,[9] it is appropriate to name them in the abstract as well as in the title. This will help readers who are interested in locating research on the characteristics of specific measures. In Example 3.3.3, mentioning the name of a specific measure is appropriate because the focus of the research is the measure.

### Example 3.3.3
*Excerpt from an abstract that provides the title of a measure (appropriate because the purpose of the research is to investigate the measure)*:

Test-retest reliability of the Test of Variables of Attention (T.O.V.A.) was investigated in two studies using two different time intervals: 90 min and 1 week (2 days). To investigate the 90-min reliability, 31 school-age children (M = 10 years, SD = 2.66) were administered the T.O.V.A. then re-administered the test....

## ___ 4. Are the highlights of the results described?

Very satisfactory   5   4   3   2   1   Very unsatisfactory   *or*   N/A   I/I

*Comment*: Example 3.4.1 shows the last two sentences of an abstract, which describe the highlights of the results of a study. Notice that the researchers make general statements about their results, such as "more likely," without stating how much more likely (e.g., twice as likely). General statements of this type are acceptable given the need for

---

[9] Researchers usually refer to measurement tools such as tests, interview protocols, and questionnaires as *instruments*.

brevity in an abstract. In other words, it is acceptable to point out only general highlights of the results.

### Example 3.4.1[10]

*Last two sentences of abstract (highlights of results reported):*

Findings suggest that Asian students are more likely than Caucasian students to believe women should be held responsible for preventing rape and to view sex as the primary motivation for rape. Asians also have stronger beliefs than Caucasians do that victims cause the rape and that most rapists are strangers.

Note that there is nothing inherently wrong with providing specific results in an abstract if space permits and if they are not misleading out of the context of the full research report. Example 3.4.2 illustrates this. First, the researcher notes that three themes "predominated," which suggests a majority noted these themes. Then there is mention of a specific statistic: "one-third." Notice, however, that the author still is citing only highlights, for instance, by using the phrase "by at least one-third" rather than stating the specific fraction (or associated percentage) for each of the three additional themes.

### Example 3.4.2[11]

*Part of an abstract with some specific results reported as highlights:*

Interviews with a diverse group of juniors and seniors from three secondary schools in the northeastern United States revealed substantial agreement in their images of America. Three themes predominated: inequality associated with race, gender, socioeconomic status, or disability; freedom including rights and opportunities; and diversity based on race, ethnicity, culture, and geography. Three additional themes were voiced by at least one-third of the students: America as better than other nations, progress, and the American dream. Crosscutting these themes were a sense of individualism or personalization and....

## ___ 5. If the study is strongly tied to a theory, is the theory mentioned in the abstract?

Very satisfactory   5   4   3   2   1   Very unsatisfactory   *or*   N/A   I/I

*Comment*: As you know from the last chapter, a theory that is central to a study might be mentioned in the title. If such a theory is not mentioned in the title, it should be mentioned in the abstract, as illustrated in Example 3.5.1. It is also acceptable to men-

---

[10] Lee, J., Pomeroy, E. C., Yoo, S.-K., & Rheinboldt, K. T. (2005). Attitudes toward rape: A comparison between Asian and Caucasian college students. *Violence Against Women, 11,* 177–196.

[11] Cornbleth, C. (2002). Images of America: What youth *do* know about the United States. *American Educational Research Journal, 39,* 519–552.

tion it in both the title and abstract, as illustrated in Example 3.5.2. (Note that bold italics have been used in these examples for emphasis.)

### Example 3.5.1[12]

*Title and abstract in which two specific theories are named in the abstract but not the title (acceptable to deemphasize theory)*:

*Title*: Exploring Work and Family Distractions: Antecedents and Outcomes

*Abstract*: Drawing from ***expansionist theory*** and ***time-based role-conflict theory***, this research investigated antecedents and outcomes of time spent in 1 role while distracted or preoccupied by another role. Survey data from a sample of 171 working mothers generally supported hypotheses linking work and family distractions to role quality. Work-role overload was positively related to work distractions experienced at home, and traditional gender-role expectations were positively related to family distractions experienced at work. In terms of outcomes, work distractions at home were negatively related to job satisfaction. Results illustrate the importance of role quality and the efficacy of alternate operationalizations of role time in the effort to better understand the interface between work and family.

### Example 3.5.2[13]

*Title and abstract in which a specific theory is mentioned in the title and abstract (acceptable to emphasize theory)*:

*Title*: Testing ***Self-Focused Attention Theory*** in Clinical Supervision: Effects of Supervisee Anxiety and Performance

*Abstract*: Audio- or videotaping and one-way mirrors are often used in clinical supervision. Yet, the effects of audio- or videotaping on supervisees have yielded equivocal results. Some studies suggest that audio- or videotaping increases trainee anxiety and hinders performance, whereas other studies suggest negligible effects. The authors present two studies in which they tested ***self-focused attention theory*** (e.g., C. S. Carver & M. F. Scheier, 1982; S. Duval & R. A. Wicklund, 1972) to explain the equivocal findings. In each study, trainees were randomly assigned to one of three awareness conditions (private or public self-awareness, or subjective awareness) and conducted initial counseling sessions. Analyses of supervisee anxiety and performance found no significant differences due to self-awareness condition in either study. The results suggest that a mirror and audio- or videotaping elicit trivial aversive effects on supervisees.

---

[12]Cardenas, R. A., Major, D. A., & Bernas, K. H. (2004). Exploring work and family distractions: Antecedents and outcomes. *International Journal of Stress Management, 11*, 346–365.
[13]Ellis, M. V., Krengel, M., & Beck, M. (2002). Testing self-focused attention theory in clinical supervision: Effects of supervisee anxiety and performance. *Journal of Counseling Psychology, 49*, 101–116.

### ___ 6. Has the researcher avoided making vague references to implications and future research directions?

Very satisfactory  5  4  3  2  1  Very unsatisfactory  *or*  N/A  I/I

*Comment*: Most researchers discuss the implications of their research and directions for future research near the end of their research reports. However, the limited amount of space allotted to abstracts should not be used to make vague references to these matters. Example 3.6.1 is the closing sentence from an abstract. It contains vague references to implications and future research.

### Example 3.6.1

*Last sentence of an abstract with vague references to implications and future research (inappropriate)*:

This article concludes with a discussion of both the implications of the results and directions for future research.

Example 3.6.1 could safely be omitted from the abstract without causing a loss of important information because most readers will correctly assume that most research reports discuss these elements. An alternative is to state something specific about these matters, as illustrated in Example 3.6.2. Notice that in this example, the researcher does not describe the implications but tells us something specific: The implications will be of special interest to a particular group of professionals—school counselors. This will alert school counselors that this research report (among the many hundreds of others on drug abuse) might be of special interest to them. If space does not permit such a long closing sentence in the abstract, it could be shortened to "Implications for school counselors are discussed."[14]

### Example 3.6.2

*Improved version of Example 3.6.1 (last sentence of an abstract)*:

While these results have implications for all professionals who work with adolescents who abuse drugs, special attention is given to the implications for school counselors.

In short, implications and future research do not necessarily need to be mentioned in abstracts. If they are mentioned, however, something specific should be said about them.

---

[14] Note that this statement would not be needed if it appeared in an abstract in a journal with a title such as *Research in School Counseling* because it would be reasonable to expect that all research reports in such a journal would contain discussions of implications for school counselors. Hence, it is not necessary to refer to implications in an abstract unless the researcher can say something about the implications that adds information and helps consumers of research locate articles appropriate to their interests.

___ **7. Overall, is the abstract effective and appropriate?**

Very satisfactory   5   4   3   2   1   Very unsatisfactory   *or*   N/A   I/I

*Comment*: Rate this evaluation question after considering your answers to the earlier ones in this chapter and any additional considerations and concerns you may have. Be prepared to rewrite the abstracts of research reports to which you assign low ratings.

When answering this evaluation question, also consider whether all three major elements are included in an abstract. Example 3.7.1 shows the three elements in bold.

### Example 3.7.1[15]

*An abstract with the three major elements indicated in bold*:

**Purpose**: This study examined the effects of gender, ethnicity, and medical illness on cessation of alcohol consumption in late life by analyzing characteristics that distinguish current drinkers from former drinkers. **Method**: Participants were 211 medical patients aged 55 to 91 years, recruited from four urban public sector primary care clinics. Respondents completed an alcohol screening test and provided health and demographic data. **Results**: Older age, hypertension, and heart problems were associated with drinking cessation among women but not among men. In a logistic regression model, drinking cessation was predicted by being unmarried, being a member of an ethnic minority group, heart problems, and diabetes.

# Exercise for Chapter 3

## Part A

*Directions*: Evaluate each of the following abstracts (to the extent that it is possible to do so without reading the associated articles) by answering Evaluation Question 7 (Overall, is the abstract effective and appropriate?) using a scale from 1 (very unsatisfactory) to 5 (very satisfactory). In the explanations for your ratings, refer to the other evaluation questions in this chapter.

References for the following abstracts are given in the footnotes. The journals in which they appeared are widely available in large academic libraries, making it possible for you to consult the complete articles if they are assigned by your instructor. More definitive application of the evaluation criteria for abstracts is possible by first reading complete articles and then evaluating their abstracts.

---

[15] Based on an abstract by Satre, D. D., & Areán, P. A. (2005). Effects of gender, ethnicity, and medical illness on drinking cessation in older primary care patients. *Journal of Aging and Health, 17*, 70–84.

1. *Title*: An Investigation into the Relationship Between Effective Administrative Leadership Styles and the Use of Technology[16]

*Abstract*: Advances in technology have inspired a growing debate regarding effective instructional strategies in our present educational system. As the roles and responsibilities of administrative leaders shift, this research was conducted to ascertain what leadership attributes affect the integration of technology to improve teaching and learning. A survey of Ohio public educators was conducted to identify faculty perceptions of building leadership and how these perceptions influence attitudes toward innovative technology implementation efforts, and ultimately student achievement. This study focuses on the relationship between administrative leadership styles and implementation of new technological programs or instructional strategies.

Overall, is the abstract effective and appropriate?

5    4    3    2    1

Explain your rating:


2. *Title*: Belief, Optimism and Caring: Findings from a Cross-National Study of Expertise in Mental Health Social Work[17]

*Abstract*: What characterizes expertise in mental health social work? This article attempts to answer this question by reporting on the findings of a cross-national Australian and American study of social work practice expertise in mental health settings, particularly in working with people with long-term serious mental illness. The study identified expert practitioners through a peer-nomination process and asked each of them to describe a memorable practice situation in focus groups. These group interviews were transcribed verbatim and analyzed using a constant comparative method. In the face of often complex and demanding work situations, these social workers demonstrated qualities specific to mental health social work that were designated as belief, optimism and caring. These three qualities are delineated and discussed in this article, as well as the implications for social work practice and education.

Overall, is the abstract effective and appropriate?

5    4    3    2    1

Explain your rating:

---

[16] Hughes, M., & Zachariah, S. (2001). An investigation into the relationship between effective administrative leadership styles and the use of technology. *International Electronic Journal for Leadership in Learning, 5*. Retrieved from http://www.acs.ucalgary.ca/~iejll/ on December 15, 2002.

[17] Ryan, M., Merighi, J. R., Healy, B., & Renouf, N. (2004). Belief, optimism and caring: Findings from a cross-national study of expertise in mental health social work. *Qualitative Social Work, 3*, 411–429.

3. *Title*: Wrong Side of the Tracks: Exploring the Role of Newspaper Coverage of Homicide in Socially Constructing Dangerous Places[18]

*Abstract*: While much research has been conducted concerning the coverage of crime by the media, little is known about the spatial aspect of this coverage. Specifically, media research has failed to determine whether the coverage of crime by the media is truly representative of where crime occurs, or whether media coverage presents crime as occurring disproportionately in certain areas of a city. Building on earlier research, and utilizing an exhaustive spatial data set and advanced spatial statistics, this research attempts to determine the degree to which newspaper coverage of homicide is spatially representative of the true homicide picture. Findings indicate that actual homicide hot spots near the city center are more likely to be covered than those on the periphery of the city and that celebrated news coverage is focused largely within the city center. In addition to trends in the spatial coverage of homicides, important social implications relating to fear of crime will be discussed.

Overall, is the abstract effective and appropriate?

5   4   3   2   1

Explain your rating:

4. *Title*: Explaining Potential Antecedents of Workplace Social Support: Reciprocity or Attractiveness?[19]

*Abstract*: Effects of social support are an important topic in occupational stress theories and research, yet little is known about support's potential antecedents. Based on reciprocity theory, the authors hypothesized that the social support received is related to the extent the employee performs organizational citizenship behaviors directed at individuals and to one's social competence; based on the notion of personal attraction, the authors hypothesized that employees' physical attractiveness and sense of humor would be associated with the amount of social support received. In a survey of 123 high school employees and separate ratings of their attractiveness, reciprocity variables were related but attraction variables were not related to social support availability. Further research should examine reciprocity in predicting social support.

Overall, is the abstract effective and appropriate?

5   4   3   2   1

Explain your rating:

---

[18] Paulsen. D. J. (2002). Wrong side of the tracks: Exploring the role of newspaper coverage of homicide in socially constructing dangerous places. *Journal of Criminal Justice and Popular Culture*, 9, 113–127.
[19] Bowling, N. A. et al. (2004). Explaining potential antecedents of workplace social support: Reciprocity or attractiveness? *Journal of Occupational Health Psychology*, 9, 339–350.

5. *Title*: Psychological Reactions to Redress: Diversity Among Japanese Americans Interned During World War II[20]

*Abstract*: The psychological reactions of 2nd-generation (Nisei) Japanese Americans to receiving redress from the U.S. government for the injustices of their World War II internment were investigated. The respondents, all of whom had been interned during the war, rated the degree to which the receipt of redress nearly 50 years after their incarceration was associated with eight different areas of personal impact. Results indicated that redress was reported to be most effective in increasing faith in the government and least effective in reducing physical suffering from the internment. Women and older respondents reported more positive redress effects. In addition, lower levels of current income, an attitudinal preference for Japanese Americans, and preredress support for seeking monetary compensation each increased the prediction of positive redress effects. Findings are discussed in relation to theories of social and retributive justice.

Overall, is the abstract effective and appropriate?

5    4    3    2    1

Explain your rating:

6. *Title*: Changes Over Time in Teenage Sexual Relationships: Comparing the High School Class of 1950, 1975, and 2000[21]

*Abstract*: This study investigated the sexual attitudes and experiences in adolescence of 242 individuals who graduated from the same high school in the northeastern United States over a 50-year period. Specifically, a survey was mailed to members of the class of 1950, the class of 1975, and the class of 2000 to examine changes over time. Overall findings suggest a significant change in sexual attitudes and experiences when comparing the class of 1950 to the classes of 1975 and 2000.

Overall, is the abstract effective and appropriate?

5    4    3    2    1

Explain your rating:

---

[20] Nagata, D. K., & Takeshita, Y. J. (2002). Psychological reactions to redress: Diversity among Japanese Americans interned during World War II. *Cultural Diversity and Ethnic Minority Psychology, 8*, 41–59.

[21] Caron, S. L., & Moskey, E. G. (2002). Changes over time in teenage sexual relationships: Comparing the high school class of 1950, 1975, and 2000. *Adolescence, 37*, 515–526.

7. *Title*: Development and Validation of a Modified Version of the Peritraumatic Dissociative Experiences Questionnaire [22]

*Abstract*: This article reports results from three studies conducted to develop and validate a modified version of the self-administered form of the Peritraumatic Dissociative Experiences Questionnaire (PDEQ; C. R. Marmar, D. S. Weiss, & T. J. Metzler, 1997). The objective was to develop an instrument suitable for use with persons from diverse ethnic and socioeconomic backgrounds. In Study 1, the original PDEQ was administered to a small sample ($N = 15$) recruited from men admitted to the hospital for physical injuries stemming from exposure to community violence. Results led to modifications aimed at improving the utility of the instrument. In Study 2, the modified PDEQ was subjected to structural equation modeling and item response theory analyses to assess its psychometric properties in a larger, primarily male, sample of community violence survivors ($N = 284$). In Study 3, the reliability and validity of the modified instrument were further assessed in a sample of female survivors of sexual assault ($N = 90$). Results attest to the psychometric properties as well as the reliability and validity of the modified 8-item PDEQ.

Overall, is the abstract effective and appropriate?

5   4   3   2   1

Explain your rating:

## Part B

*Directions*: Examine several academic journals that publish on topics of interest to you. Identify two with abstracts that you think are especially strong in terms of the evaluation questions presented in this chapter. Also, identify two abstracts that clearly have weaknesses. Bring the four abstracts to class for discussion.

---

[22] Marshall, G. N., Orlando, M., Jaycox, L. H., Foy, D. W., & Belzberg, H. (2002). Development and validation of a modified version of the peritraumatic dissociative experiences questionnaire. *Psychological Assessment, 14*, 123–134.

# Chapter 4

# Evaluating Introductions and Literature Reviews

Research reports in academic journals usually begin with an Introduction in which literature is cited.[1] An integrated Introduction and literature review has these five purposes: (a) introduce the problem area, (b) establish its importance, (c) provide an overview of the relevant literature, (d) show how the current study will advance knowledge in the area, and (e) describe the researcher's specific research questions, purposes, or hypotheses, which usually are stated in the last paragraph of the introduction.

This chapter presents evaluation questions regarding the introductory material in a research report. In the next chapter, the evaluation of the literature review portion is considered.

## ____ 1. Does the researcher begin by identifying a specific problem area?

Very satisfactory   5   4   3   2   1   Very unsatisfactory   *or*   N/A   I/I

*Comment*: Some researchers start their Introductions with statements that are so broad they fail to identify the specific area of investigation. As the beginning of an Introduction to a study on the effects of smoking and obesity, Example 4.1.1 is deficient. Notice that it fails to identify the specific areas of public health that are explored in the research.

### Example 4.1.1
*Beginning of an inappropriately broad Introduction*:

State and local governments expend considerable resources for research on public health issues. The findings of this research are used to formulate public policies that regulate health-related activities within the broader society. In addition to helping establish regulations, public health agencies attempt to educate the public so that individuals have appropriate information when making individual lifestyle decisions that may affect their health.

---

[1] In theses and dissertations, the first chapter usually is an Introduction, with relatively few references to the literature. This is followed by a chapter that provides a comprehensive literature review.

Example 4.1.2 illustrates a more appropriate beginning for a research report on the relative risks of smoking and obesity to health.

### Example 4.1.2[2]

*A specific beginning (compare with Example 4.1.1)*:

Cigarette smoking and obesity are both widespread and significant health liabilities that increase the risks of hypertension, ischemic heart disease, noninsulin-dependent diabetes, and various types of cancer. Objectively, the relative risks associated with smoking outstrip those associated with obesity (U.S. Department of Health and Human Services, 1990). At most weight levels, smokers suffer nearly twice the mortality of nonsmokers from cancer, heart disease, stroke, and diabetes (VanItallie, 1992). The mortality associated with being overweight approaches the mortality associated with smoking only when weight exceeds 110% of desirable, healthy body weight (Hahn, Teutsch, Rothenberg, & Marks, 1990; VanItallie, 1992).

Making a decision as to whether a researcher has started the Introduction by being reasonably specific often involves some subjectivity. As a general rule, the researcher should get to the point quickly without using valuable journal space to outline a very broad problem area rather than the specific one(s) that he or she has directly studied.

### ____ 2. Does the researcher establish the importance of the problem area?

Very satisfactory   5   4   3   2   1   Very unsatisfactory   *or*   N/A   I/I

*Comment*: Researchers select research problems they believe are important, and they should specifically address this belief early in their Introductions. Often, this is done by citing previously published statistics that indicate how widespread a problem is, how many people are affected by it, and so on. Example 4.2.1 illustrates how one researcher did this in the first paragraph of a study on the effectiveness of an educational program for incarcerated adults with disabilities. Note that there are many hundreds of studies on incarceration (numbers who are incarcerated, ethnicity of the incarcerated, effects of various forms of punishment, legal issues regarding incarceration, ethical and political issues regarding capital punishment, and so on). However, the authors of Example 4.2.1 avoid muddling their Introduction with information on numerous related issues. Instead, they focus immediately on academic achievement and the dis-

---

[2] Johnsen, L., Spring, B., Pingitore, R., Sommerfeld, B. K., & MacKirnan, D. (2002). Smoking as subculture? Influence on Hispanic and non-Hispanic White women's attitudes toward smoking and obesity. *Health Psychology, 21*, 279–287.

abled, citing specific statistics (e.g., "only half" and "two-thirds") to justify their study.

### Example 4.2.1[3]

*First paragraph of an Introduction that includes statistics to establish the importance of a problem area*:

Accumulating evidence suggests that low academic achievement is a major factor in crime (Farnworth & Leiber, 1989; Williamson, 1992). According to the Bureau of Justice Statistics (2000), only half of the inmates in federal, state, or local jails have a high school diploma or its equivalent, a third have a mental or physical disability, and almost two-thirds were unemployed during the month before their arrest. Research also shows that inmates with special education needs are overrepresented in juvenile and adult correctional facilities (Fink, 1990; Rutherford, Nelson, & Wolford, 1985; Morgan, 1979; Winters, 1997). The disproportionate number of students with an emotional or learning disability who drop out of school most likely adds to these numbers (Phelps & Hanley-Maxwell, 1997).

Example 4.2.2 also uses statistical information to justify the importance of a study on marital violence and its effects on children.

### Example 4.2.2[4]

*Beginning of an Introduction that includes statistical information to establish the importance of a problem area*:

Marital violence is a ubiquitous and pressing social concern. Nearly 30% of married couples experience spousal violence at some point during their marriage, and with correction for underreporting, this estimate could be as high as 50% (Straus, Gelles, & Steinmetz, 1980). Physical violence not only corrodes the fabric of the marital relationship but also impacts children living in these homes. By some estimates, approximately 3 million children witness interparental violence each year (Carlson, 1984).

Instead of providing statistics on the prevalence of problems, researchers sometimes use other strategies to convince readers of the importance of the research problems they studied. One approach is to show that a topic is of current interest because of corporate or government actions, such as the passage of the Americans with Disabilities Act. Another is to show that prominent people or influential authors have

---

[3] Bottge, B. A., & Watson, E. A. (2002). Using video-based math problems to connect the skills and understandings of incarcerated adults with disabilities. *Journal of Special Education Technology, 17*. No page numbers given. The example appears on the first page of this URL, which is maintained by the journal: http://jset.unlv.edu/17.2/bottge/first.html. Retrieved December 12, 2002.

[4] Katz, L. F., & Low, S. M. (2004). Marital violence, co-parenting, and family-level processes in relation to children's adjustment. *Journal of Family Psychology, 18*, 372–382.

considered and addressed the issue that is being researched. Example 4.2.3 illustrates the latter technique. The names of influential people in the example are in bold for emphasis.

> **Example 4.2.3**[5]
>
> *Excerpt from an Introduction that uses a nonstatistical argument to establish the importance of a problem*:
>
> In addition to our fascination with individual-level happiness, we have become especially interested in the last few hundred years in determining what makes the group happy too. Influential thinkers such as **Jeremy Bentham** and **John Stuart Mill** have argued that we should seek the greatest good for the greatest number. In a similar vein, Murray (1988) traces the adoption of happiness as the ultimate goal for government, quoting notable American historical figures such as **James Madison**, **John Adams**, and **George Washington**. Such is its acceptance that the United States Declaration of Independence has the sentiment enshrined: "We hold these truths to be self-evident, that all men are created equal, that they are endowed by their Creator with certain unalienable Rights, that among these are Life, Liberty and *the pursuit of Happiness* [italics added]."

Finally, a researcher may attempt to establish the nature and importance of a problem by citing anecdotal evidence or personal experience. While this is arguably the weakest way to establish the importance of a problem, a unique and interesting anecdote might convince readers that the problem is important enough to investigate.

*A caveat*: When you apply Evaluation Question 2 to the Introduction of a research report, do *not* confuse the importance of a problem with your personal interest in the problem. It is possible to have little personal interest in a problem yet still recognize that a researcher has established its importance. On the other hand, it is possible to have a strong personal interest in a problem but judge that the researcher has failed to make a strong argument (or has failed to present convincing evidence) to establish its importance.

## ____ 3. Are any underlying theories adequately described?

Very satisfactory   5   4   3   2   1   Very unsatisfactory   *or*   N/A   I/I

*Comment*: Much useful research is *nontheoretical*. Sometimes, the purpose of a study is simply to collect and interpret data in order to make a practical decision. For instance, a researcher might poll parents to determine what percentage favors a proposed new regulation that would require students to wear uniforms when attending school.

---

[5] Steel, P., & Ones, D. S. (2002). Personality and happiness: A national-level analysis. *Journal of Personality and Social Psychology, 83*, 767–781.

Nontheoretical information on parents' attitudes toward requiring uniforms might be an important consideration when a school board is making a decision on the issue.

Another major reason for conducting nontheoretical research is to determine whether there is a problem and/or the incidence of the problem. For instance, a researcher might collect data on the percentage of pregnant women attending a county medical clinic who use tobacco products during pregnancy. The resulting data will help decision makers determine how important this problem is within the clinic's population, which might have implications for the amount of emphasis to place on tobacco cessation programs at the clinic. Simply determining the incidence of tobacco use in this population does not require a theoretical basis for the research.

When applying Evaluation Question 3 to nontheoretical research, "not applicable" (N/A) will usually be the best answer. However, if a theory is alluded to or specifically named in the Introduction to a research article, the theory or theories should be adequately described. Deciding whether it is adequately described can be highly subjective because well-known theories need not be described in great detail while newer, emerging theories should be described in much greater detail. As a general rule, even a well-known theory should be described in at least a short paragraph (along with one or more references where additional information can be found) for readers who may be new to the field. Note that if the explicit, stated purpose of research is to test a proposition or prediction based on a theory, one would expect the theory to be discussed in detail even if it is well known.

Example 4.3.1 briefly but clearly summarizes the theory of conservation of resources (COR) theory, which was a basis for the research on strain among low-income mothers. Note that the researchers specifically address how the theory might apply to this particular group.[6]

### Example 4.3.1[7]

*Excerpt from the Introduction to a research article that describes a theory that underlies the research*:

COR theory is a general theory of human motivation based on the supposition that people strive to retain, protect, and build resources and that the potential or actual loss of these valued resources is seen as a threat. According to COR theory, women low in resources are likely to experience elevated levels of role strain, as they are likely to perceive the multiple responsibilities associated with motherhood and employment as a threat to their already meager resources. In contrast, women high in resources are less likely to feel threatened by the multiple demands of motherhood and employment than to feel that they possess the needed resources to successfully meet the demands of their multiple roles.

---

[6] Only a brief excerpt of the discussion of how the theory might apply is shown in the example.
[7] Morris, J. E., & Coley, R. L. (2004). Maternal, family, and work correlates of role strain in low-income mothers. *Journal of Family Psychology, 18*, 424–432.

*A special note for evaluating qualitative research*: Often, qualitative researchers explore problem areas without initial reference to theories and hypotheses based on them. Instead, they develop theories (and models and other generalizations) as they collect and analyze data. The data often take the form of transcripts from open-ended interviews, notes on direct observation and participation in activities with participants, and so on. Thus, in a research article reporting on qualitative research, a theory might not be described until the Results and Discussion sections (instead of the Introduction). When this is the case, apply Evaluation Question 3 at the point at which theory is discussed.

## ___ 4. Does the Introduction move from topic to topic instead of from citation to citation?

Very satisfactory   5   4   3   2   1   Very unsatisfactory   *or*   N/A   I/I

*Comment*: Introductions that typically fail on this evaluation question are organized around citations rather than topics. For instance, a researcher might inappropriately first summarize Smith's study, then summarize Jones's study, then summarize Doe's study, and so on. The result is a series of annotations that are merely strung together. This fails to guide readers through the literature and fails to show how the various references relate to each other and what they mean as a whole.

In contrast, an Introduction should be organized around topics and subtopics with references cited as needed, often in groups of two or more citations to literature. For instance, if four research reports support a certain point, the point usually should be stated with all four references cited together (as opposed to writing a separate statement or paragraph for each of the four references).

In Example 4.4.1 below, there are two citations to *reviews* of literature to support the beneficial effects of regular exercise. Presumably, reviews are potentially more valid sources because they represent a body of findings—not just the findings of individual studies. Also, note that there are two other groups of two citations (cited together within parentheses) within the example, such as the one in the last sentence.

### Example 4.4.1[8]

*An excerpt from a literature review with references cited in groups*:

Research indicates that regular exercise has favorable effects on mental health, self-esteem, and sense of overall well-being (see U.S. Department of Health and Human Services, 1996; Morgan, 1997, for reviews). It has been cited as useful for treating psychological disorders such as depression (Craft & Landers, 1998) and anxiety (Martinsen, 1993; Landers & Petruzzello, 1994), as well as providing prophylactic effects (Plante, 1993). Exercise improves psychological states

---

[8] Annesi, J. J. (2002). Relation of rated fatigue and changes in energy after exercise and over 14 weeks in previously sedentary women exercisers. *Perceptual and Motor Skills, 95,* 719–727.

in individuals already within "normal" ranges; however, those with the most unfavorable emotional states may benefit most (North, McCullah, & Tran, 1990; Petruzzello, Landers, Hatfield, Kubitz, & Salazar, 1991).

Of course, when a researcher is discussing a reference that is crucial to a point he or she is making, that reference should be discussed in more detail than was done in Example 4.4.1. However, because research reports in academic journals are expected to be relatively brief, this should be done sparingly and only for the most important related literature.

## ___ 5. Is the Introduction a coherent essay with logical transitions from topic to topic?

Very satisfactory   5   4   3   2   1   Very unsatisfactory   *or*   N/A   I/I

*Comment*: When there are a number of issues to be covered in a long Introduction, there may be several essays, each with its own subheading, which help guide readers. Each of the paragraphs normally should have the typical organization with a topic idea (often stated in the first sentence) that is enlarged on and supported by details (usually citations to previous research). Transitions from one paragraph to the next should be logical. Often, researchers do this by starting paragraphs with transitional terms, as illustrated in Example 4.5.1, which deals with the role of the media in shaping public perceptions of the president of the United States.

### Example 4.5.1[9]
*The beginnings of six paragraphs from an Introduction to research (paragraphs 2 through 6 begin with transitional terms, which are shown in italics for emphasis)*:

Research has shown that news coverage can focus public attention on particular topics and, in so doing, alter the mix of cognitions that are most readily accessible when forming political judgments (Dalton, Beck, and Huckfeldt, 1998)....

*Consistent with this work*, yet adopting a longitudinal perspective, Pan and Kosicki (1997) suggest that research on public opinion needs to pay closer attention to....

*In particular*, economic news coverage—specifically, emphasis upon favorable or unfavorable developments or indicators—may help shape evaluations of presidential job performance because....

*Consistent with this view*, Hetherington (1996) found that the quantity of political information consumed by citizens....

---

[9] Shah, D. V., Watts, M. D., Domke, D., & Fan, D. P. (2002). News framing and cueing of issue regimes: Explaining Clinton's public approval in spite of scandal. *Public Opinion Quarterly*, *66*, 339–370.

*Similarly*, research suggests that coverage of a president's general performance on policy issues plays a key role in molding approval ratings (Brody, 1991). Iyengar and colleagues (see Iyengar, 1991; Iyengar and Kinder, 1987) have suggested that news....

*In addition*, scholars have distinguished between the private and public aspects of political performance—that is, "between the personal and the presidential" (Jamieson, 1998, p. 21; also Lawrence, Bennett, and Hunt, 1999). This distinction suggests that....

## ___ 6. Has the researcher provided conceptual definitions of key terms?

Very satisfactory  5  4  3  2  1  Very unsatisfactory  *or*  N/A  I/I

*Comment*: Often, researchers will pause at appropriate points in their Introductions to offer formal conceptual definitions,[10] such as the one shown in Example 4.6.1. Note that it is acceptable for a researcher to cite a previously published definition—in this case, one proposed by Barber et al. Also, note that the researchers contrast the term being defined (i.e., psychological control) with a term with which it might be confused (i.e., behavioral control), which is a desirable technique.

### Example 4.6.1[11]

*A conceptual definition provided in an Introduction to a research report*:

One characteristic of parenting that has recently gained increasing attention is *psychological control*, defined as parental behaviors that are intrusive and manipulative of children's thoughts, feelings, and attachments to parents (Barber, 1996; Barber & Harmon, 2002). According to Barber, Olsen, and Shagle (1994), the distinction between behavioral and psychological forms of control lies in the focus of the attempt at control: Whereas behavioral control is an attempt to regulate the child's behavior, psychological control focuses on exercising control over the child's psychological world. It has been assumed that psychological control stems from parents' intrapsychic need to protect their "psychological power" in the parent-child relationship, whereas behavioral control is motivated by parents' attempts to socialize their children (Barber & Harmon, 2002; Pettit et al., 2001).

Conceptual definitions do not need to be lengthy as long as their meaning is clear. Example 4.6.2 shows a brief conceptual definition.

---

[10] A *conceptual definition* seeks to identify a term using only general concepts but with enough specificity that the term is not confused with other related terms or concepts. As such, it resembles dictionary definitions. In contrast, an *operational definition* describes the physical process used to examine a variable.

[11] Aunola, K., & Nurmi, J.-E. (2004). Maternal affection moderates the impact of psychological control on a child's mathematical performance. *Developmental Psychology, 40*, 965–978.

**Example 4.6.2**[12]

*A conceptual definition provided in an Introduction to a research report*:

Resilience has recently been defined as the capacity of those exposed to risk factors to overcome these risks and avoid negative outcomes by engaging in competent behavior (Rak & Patterson, 1996; Serbin & Stack, 1998).

At times, researchers may not provide formal definitions, but you might judge that the terms have such widespread commonly held definitions that they do not need to be defined in the research articles. For example, in a report of research on various methods of teaching handwriting, a researcher may not offer a definition of handwriting in his or her Introduction, and you might judge this to be acceptable. Of course, you will expect the researcher to describe later how handwriting was measured (i.e., the *operational definition*; see footnote 10 in this chapter) when you get to the details of the methods used to conduct the research. Note that the Method section of a research report typically follows the Introduction and literature review.

In sum, this evaluation question should not be applied mechanically by looking to see if there is a specific statement of a definition. The mere absence of one does not necessarily mean that a researcher has failed on this evaluation question because you may judge that a definition simply is not needed. When this is the case, you may give the research a rating of N/A ("not applicable") for this evaluation question.

## ___ 7. Has the researcher indicated the basis for "factual" statements?

Very satisfactory  5  4  3  2  1  Very unsatisfactory  *or*  N/A  I/I

*Comment*: Researchers should avoid making statements that sound like "facts" without referring to their source. As you know from freshman composition, this is highly undesirable. A common statement of this type is the unsubstantiated claim that interest in a problem is growing or that the number of people affected by a problem is increasing, which is illustrated in Example 4.7.1. Notice that not only is the "fact" not substantiated with a reference to its source, it is also vague because "dramatically" is not defined. Example 4.7.2 is an improved version.

**Example 4.7.1**

*An unreferenced "factual" claim*:

Interest in child abuse and mistreatment has increased dramatically in recent years.

---

[12] Fiorentino, L., & Howe, N. (2004). Language competence, narrative ability, and school readiness in low-income preschool children. *Canadian Journal of Behavioural Science, 36*, 280–294.

**Example 4.7.2**[13]

*A referenced "fact" (compare with Example 4.7.1):*

Child maltreatment incident reports increased by 50% between 1988 and 1993, totaling more than 2.9 million reports in 1993 (McCurdy & Daro, 1994). Much of this increase can be attributed to....

Note, however, that it is appropriate for researchers to express their opinions in Introductions as long as the context makes it clear that they are opinions and not "facts." In Example 4.7.3, the researcher expresses what is clearly an opinion because of his/her use of the word "presumption."

**Example 4.7.3**[14]

*A statement properly identified as an opinion:*

The presumption here is that literacy is context sensitive; that is, varied contexts (economic, cultural, gendered, geographical, historical, ideological, linguistic, racial/ethnic, religious, and social) affect access to literacy and opportunity for its development and use. Given these considerations, equal outcomes should not be expected from unequal circumstances.

## ___ 8. Do the specific research purposes, questions, or hypotheses logically flow from the introductory material?

Very satisfactory  5  4  3  2  1  Very unsatisfactory  *or*  N/A  I/I

*Comment*: Typically, the specific research purposes, questions, or hypotheses that drive a research study are stated in the last paragraph of the Introduction.[15] The material preceding them should set the stage and logically lead to them. For instance, if a researcher argues that research methods used by previous researchers are not well suited for answering certain research questions, you would not be surprised to learn that his or her research purpose is to reexamine the research questions using alternative research methods. Likewise, if a researcher points out in the Introduction that there are certain specific gaps in what is known about a problem area (i.e., the previously published literature has not covered certain subtopics), you would not be surprised to learn that the purpose of the study that is being introduced is designed to fill those gaps. In Example 4.8.1, which is the last paragraph in the Introduction to a research report, the researchers provide a very brief statement on the literature that they

---

[13] Akin, B. A., & Gregoire, T. K. (1997). Parents' views on child welfare's response to addiction. *Families in Society: The Journal of Contemporary Human Services, 78*, 393–404.

[14] Willis, A. I. (2002). Literacy at Calhoun Colored School: 1892–1945. *Reading Research Quarterly, 37*, 8–44.

[15] Some researchers state their research purposes, questions, or hypotheses in general terms near the beginning of their Introductions and then restate them more specifically near the end.

reviewed in the Introduction. This sets the stage for the specific research purposes, which are stated in the last sentence of the example.

### Example 4.8.1[16]

*Last paragraph of an Introduction (beginning with a summary of the research that was reviewed and ending with a statement of the purposes of the current research)*:

Most of the work supporting these models [reviewed above] to date has been about comprehension of television content and not about acquisition of literacy skills or the application of reading risk status to learning associated with viewing television. In addition, descriptions of the children's home media environments and subsequent relations to literacy skill acquisition are a new facet of what is known in the literature [reviewed above]. Thus, the purposes of this article are to describe the home media environments of young children, to determine whether watching an educational television series featuring literacy content for young children could improve these children's emergent literacy skills, and to examine whether home media environments and emergent literacy skill improvements varied as a function of reading risk status.

### ___ 9. Overall, is the Introduction effective and appropriate?

Very satisfactory   5   4   3   2   1   Very unsatisfactory   *or*   N/A   I/I

*Comment*: Rate this evaluation question after considering your answers to the earlier ones in this chapter and any additional considerations and concerns you may have. Be prepared to explain your overall evaluation.

# Exercise for Chapter 4

**Part A**

*Directions*: On the next page is the Introduction to a brief research report published in an academic journal.[17] Evaluate the Introduction using the rating scales that follow it.

---

[16] Linebarger, D. L., Kosanic, A. Z., Greenwood, C. R., & Doku, N. S. (2004). Effects of viewing the television program Between the Lions on the emergent literacy skills of young children. *Journal of Educational Psychology, 96*, 297–308.

[17] Johnson, M. E., Yep, M. J., Brems, C., Theno, S. A., & Fisher, D. G. (2002). Relationship among gender, depression, and needle sharing in a sample of injection drug users. *Psychology of Addictive Behaviors, 16*, 338–341.

Needle sharing is not only prevalent (Dinwiddie, 1997) but also can occur for many reasons, including historical, legal, economic, or sociocultural factors (DesJarlais, Friedman, & Strug, 1986). Sharing may be due in part to the scarcity of sterile needles or to the economic burden of acquiring sterile needles (Koester & Hoffer, 1994; Mandell, Vlahov, Cohn, Latkin, & Oziemkowska, 1994; Watters, Estilo, Clark, & Lorvick, 1994). However, even when sterile needles are available and inexpensive, factors including apathy, social custom, a sense of urgency, and psychological distress may reduce their perceived availability or affordability (Black et al., 1986; Strathdee et al., 1997). Other factors that may be related to sharing needles include severity of drug use, psychopathology, and gender. The former variable, severity of use, has been found to be significantly correlated with the risk of sharing. Specifically, injection drug users (IDUs) who inject more frequently and who inject drug combinations are significantly more likely to use borrowed needles (Klee, Faugier, Hayes, Boulton, & Morris, 1990; Watters et al., 1994).

Level of psychopathology has been explored, and studies have revealed a consistently positive relationship between needle sharing and psychiatric symptoms, especially depression (Hawkins, Latkin, Chowdury, & Hawkins, 1998; Mandell, Kim, Latkin, & Suh, 1999; Strathdee et al., 1997). Various hypotheses have attempted to explain this relationship, including the possibilities that individuals with depressive symptoms may receive needed social interaction and support from their drug network (Latkin & Mandell, 1993; Suh, Mandell, & Kim, 1997), that depression may predispose individuals toward feelings of lack of control or power (Green & Kreuter, 1991), and that depressed individuals may engage in risky health behaviors because they do not anticipate a positive future.

The relationship between sharing and gender has also received attention, with findings pointing toward an increased likelihood of sharing behavior among female IDUs (Darke, Ross, Cohen, Hando, & Hall, 1995; Wang, Siegal, Falck, & Carlson, 1998). Some of the same dynamics present among depressed individuals that may result in sharing behaviors may also be present among women. For example, Soet, Dudley, and Dilorio (1999) found that low perceived power among women affected their sexual decision-making, resulting in more risk behaviors. Although research has provided evidence that women tend to endorse higher levels of psychopathology than men (Johnson, Brems, & Fisher, 1996; McGrath, Strickland, Keita, & Russo, 1990; Rabkin et al., 1997), including higher levels of depression (Brienza et al., 2000), no study has yet explored whether gender and depression interact in their relationship with needle sharing.

Using a sample of street drug users, in the current study we examined the relationships among gender, depression, and needle sharing. We hypothesized that needle sharers would report higher levels of depression than nonsharers, that women would report higher levels of depression than men, and that female sharers would report the highest levels of depression among all other groups.

____ **1. Do the researchers begin by identifying a specific problem area?**

Very satisfactory  5  4  3  2  1  Very unsatisfactory  *or*  N/A  I/I

____ **2. Do the researchers establish the importance of the problem area?**

Very satisfactory  5  4  3  2  1  Very unsatisfactory  *or*  N/A  I/I

____ **3. Are any underlying theories adequately described?**

Very satisfactory  5  4  3  2  1  Very unsatisfactory  *or*  N/A  I/I

____ **4. Does the Introduction move from topic to topic instead of from citation to citation?**

Very satisfactory  5  4  3  2  1  Very unsatisfactory  *or*  N/A  I/I

_____ **5. Is the Introduction a coherent essay with logical transitions from topic to topic?**

Very satisfactory  5  4  3  2  1  Very unsatisfactory  *or*  N/A  I/I

_____ **6. Have the researchers provided conceptual definitions of key terms?**

Very satisfactory  5  4  3  2  1  Very unsatisfactory  *or*  N/A  I/I

_____ **7. Have the researchers indicated the basis for "factual" statements?**

Very satisfactory  5  4  3  2  1  Very unsatisfactory  *or*  N/A  I/I

_____ **8. Do the specific research purposes, questions, or hypotheses logically flow from the introductory material?**

Very satisfactory  5  4  3  2  1  Very unsatisfactory  *or*  N/A  I/I

_____ **9. Overall, is the Introduction effective and appropriate?**

Very satisfactory  5  4  3  2  1  Very unsatisfactory  *or*  N/A  I/I

## Part B

*Directions*: Read three research reports in academic journals on a topic of interest to you. Apply the evaluation questions in this chapter to the Introductions, and select the one to which you have given the highest ratings. Bring it to class for discussion. Be prepared to discuss its strengths and weaknesses.

*Notes*:

# Chapter 5

# A Closer Look at Evaluating Literature Reviews

As you learned in the previous chapter, literature reviews usually are integrated into the researcher's introductory statements. In that chapter, the emphasis was on the functions of the Introduction and the most salient and easy-to-evaluate characteristics of a literature review. This chapter explores the quality of literature reviews in more detail.

## ___ 1. If there is extensive literature on a topic, has the researcher been selective?

Very satisfactory  5  4  3  2  1  Very unsatisfactory  *or*  N/A  I/I

*Comment*: You may not know if the research on a topic is extensive unless you have studied the topic in detail or unless the researcher describes its breadth. Even in the absence of this information, one flaw related to this evaluation question can be spotted. Specifically, some researchers use very long strings of references to support a single point or position. This is often a sign that the researcher has not been selective in choosing research to cite.[1] Example 5.1.1 illustrates this flaw. Example 5.1.2 shows an improved version. Notice that "e.g.," (meaning "for example,") is appropriately used in Example 5.1.2.

### Example 5.1.1[2]
*Unselective referencing (inappropriate)*:

Several issues must be addressed before grade-sensitive indices can be identified. The first is how to identify expert literacy teachers. In the past, some researchers have asked teachers to identify their own competencies (Dillman, 1978; Warwick & Lininger, 1975; Hoover & Johnson, 1998; James, 2001; Kelp, 2002; Koontz, Doe, & Jones, 2002; Kibler & Loone, 2003; Stansky & Lip, 2003; First, Hadley, & Palms, 2003; Doe, 2003).

---

[1] Long strings of references for a single point are more justifiable in a thesis or dissertation, especially if the committee that is evaluating it expects a student to produce a comprehensive review to demonstrate that he or she can locate all the literature related to a topic.

[2] This example was modified from the original to illustrate an *inappropriate* technique. The original and its reference are given in Example 5.1.2.

**Example 5.1.2**[3]

*Selective referencing (citing only important references)*:

Several issues must be addressed before grade-sensitive indices can be identified. The first is how to identify expert literacy teachers. In the past, some researchers have asked teachers to assess their own competencies (e.g., Dillman, 1978; Warwick & Lininger, 1975).

## ___ 2. Is the literature review critical?

Very satisfactory   5   4   3   2   1   Very unsatisfactory   *or*   N/A   I/I

*Comment*: A researcher should consider the strengths and weaknesses of previously published studies.[4] Note that criticism can be positive (as in Example 5.2.1) in which the authors refer to "well-designed" studies.

**Example 5.2.1**[5]

*Positive criticism in a literature review*:

A number of well-designed prospective studies have found that children who are physically disciplined or maltreated are at increased risk of engaging in violent antisocial behavior in childhood and adulthood (Cicchetti & Manly, 2001; Gershoff, 2002; Lansford et al., 2002; Widom, 1989). However, other studies have shown that....

Of course, negative criticisms are often warranted. An instance of this is shown in Example 5.2.2.

**Example 5.2.2**[6]

*Negative criticism in a literature review*:

Scholars question the use of Western constructs to study parental socialization in Asian families without considering how such constructs may or may not capture meaningful behaviors among families from more collectivistic orientations (Chao, 1994; Lam, 1997). These arguments are particularly convincing given that U.S. childrearing practices originate in Western cultural traditions emphasizing personal achievement as part of an overall theme of individualism (Lam,

---

[3] Block, C. C., Oakar, M., & Hurt, N. (2002). The expertise of literacy teachers: A continuum from preschool to grade 5. *Reading Research Quarterly, 37*, 178–206.

[4] Articles based on reasonably strong methodology may be cited without comments on their strengths. However, researchers have an obligation to point out which studies are exceptionally weak. This might be done with comments such as "A small pilot study suggested...."

[5] Jaffee, S. R. et al. (2004). The limits of child effects: Evidence for genetically mediated child effects on corporal punishment but not on physical maltreatment. *Developmental Psychology, 40*, 1047–1058.

[6] Supple, A. J., Peterson, G. W., & Bush, K. R. (2004). Assessing the validity of parenting measures in a sample of Chinese adolescents. *Journal of Family Psychology, 18*, 539–544.

1997). Despite such concerns, Western measures of maternal acceptance and rejection, styles of control (Berndt, Cheung, Lau, Hau, & Lew, 1993; Steinberg, Dornbusch, & Brown, 1992; Lau & Cheung, 1987), warmth, and autonomy granting (Berndt et al., 1993; Bush, Peterson, Cobas, & Supple, 2002) have been used in studies of Chinese Americans, Chinese from Hong Kong, and Chinese from the People's Republic of China. Although the use of Western constructs and measures is common, scant evidence exists in reference to the validity of these approaches when studying adolescents from mainland China.

## ___ 3. Is current research cited?

Very satisfactory  5  4  3  2  1  Very unsatisfactory  *or*  N/A  I/I

*Comment*: You can check the currency of the literature by noting whether research published in recent years has been cited. Keep in mind, however, that relevance to the research topic is more important than currency. A ten-year-old study that is highly relevant and has superior research methodology may deserve more attention than a less relevant, methodologically weaker one that was recently published. When this is the case, the researcher should explicitly state why an older research article is being discussed in more detail than newer ones.

Also, note that a researcher may want to establish the historical context for his or her study. A historical context might help establish the legitimacy of the current studies a researcher is presenting. In Example 5.3.1, the researchers link a particular finding back to Ferster and Skinner's work in 1957. Skinner is the best known of the early behavior analysts. This is followed by references to more current literature.

### Example 5.3.1[7]

*An excerpt from a literature review showing historical links*:

Behavior analysts often allude to the imperviousness of schedule effects to particular reinforcement histories (e.g., Ferster & Skinner, 1957), but rarely is evidence adduced to substantiate that point. There is currently a small body of mixed evidence for reinforcement history effects on FI [fixed-interval] performance (Baron & Leinenweber, 1995; Cole, 2001....) For example, Wanchisen et al. (1989) found....

## ___ 4. Has the researcher distinguished between opinions and research findings?

Very satisfactory  5  4  3  2  1  Very unsatisfactory  *or*  N/A  I/I

---

[7] Ludvig, E. A., & Staddon, J. E. R. (2004). The conditions for temporal tracking under interval schedules of reinforcement. *Journal of Experimental Psychology: Animal Behavior Processes, 30*, 299–316.

*Comment*: Researchers should use wording that helps readers understand whether the cited literature presents opinions or research results.

For indicating that a citation is research based, there are a variety of options, a number of which are shown in Example 5.4.1.

### Example 5.4.1

*Examples of key terms and expressions indicating that a citation is research based*:

Recent data suggest that....

In laboratory experiments....

Recent test scores suggest....

Group A has outperformed its counterparts on measures of....

Research on XYZ has....

Data from surveys comparing....

Doe (1999) found that the rate....

These studies have greatly increased our knowledge of....

In addition, if a researcher cites a specific statistic from the literature (e.g., "In Australia, from 1991 to 2000 there was a 54% increase in higher degree research enrollments [Kemp, 2001]"[8]), it is safe to assume that research is being cited.

Sometimes, researchers cite the opinions of others. When they do this, they should word their statements in such a way that readers are made aware that opinions (and not research findings) are being cited. Example 5.4.2 shows some examples of key words and phrases that researchers sometimes use to do this.

### Example 5.4.2

*Examples of key terms and expressions indicating that an opinion is being cited*:

Jones (1999) has argued that....

These kinds of assumptions were....

Despite this speculation....

These arguments predict....

This logical suggestion....

Smith has strongly advocated the use of....

---

[8] Smith, L. (2002). Quality postgraduate research programs and student experience. *The Australian Electronic Journal of Nursing Education, 8,* accessed at http://www.scu.edu.au/schools/nhcp/aejne/vol8-1/refereed/smith_post.html on January 3, 2003.

### ___ 5. Has the researcher distinguished between what is proposed by a theory and research findings related to the theory?

Very satisfactory   5   4   3   2   1   Very unsatisfactory   *or*   N/A   I/I

*Comment*: When citing a premise from theory, a researcher should simply use the word "theory" and distinguish it from research findings related to the theory. Example 5.5.1 shows two consecutive paragraphs. The first clearly is a description of attachment theory while the second one describes research results related to the theory.

**Example 5.5.1**[9]

*Excerpt indicating the distinction between theory and research results (italics added for emphasis)*:

*According to attachment theory*, the relation between quality of early care and infant security holds across a wide range of cultures and contexts. To be clear, Bowlby (1982) proposed the attachment behavioral system to be a species-characteristic product common to all children reared within the range of our environment of evolutionary adaptedness. This can be understood as a propensity to organize an attachment behavioral system and develop an attachment relationship within the context of child–caregiver interactions (Posada et al., 1995). Further, Bowlby (1982) and Ainsworth et al. (1978) proposed that the specific quality of an attachment relationship depends on the particular history of child–caregiver interactions.

Research findings indicate that the secure-base phenomenon is common to children from different cultures and socioeconomic contexts (e.g., Ainsworth, 1967; Anderson, 1972; Posada et al., 1995). They also show that rates of secure attachment in children are lower in families under stress than in families under low-stress (usually middle-class) conditions (Posada et al., 1995; Posada et al., 1999; Valenzuela, 1990; Vaughn, Egeland, Sroufe, & Waters, 1979) and vary from culture to culture (Grossmann, Grossmann, Spangler, Suess, & Unzner, 1985; Mikaye, Chen, & Campos, 1985; Takahashi, 1986; van Ijzendoorn & Kroonenberg, 1988). These latter results regarding rates of secure and insecure attachments are not inconsistent with *attachment theory*.

### ___ 6. Has the researcher interpreted research literature in light of the inherent limits of empirical research?

Very satisfactory   5   4   3   2   1   Very unsatisfactory   *or*   N/A   I/I

---

[9] Posada, G. et al. (2002). Maternal caregiving and infant security in two cultures. *Developmental Psychology, 38*, 67–78.

*Comment*: As you know from Chapter 1, empirical research has inherent limitations. As a result, no research report offers "proof," and "facts" are rarely revealed by empirical research. Instead, research results offer *degrees of evidence*, which are sometimes extremely strong (such as the relationship between cigarette smoking and health), and much more often, are only modest or weak.

Terms that researchers can use to indicate that the results of research offer strong evidence are shown in Example 5.6.1.

**Example 5.6.1**

*Examples of terminology (in bold) that can be used to indicate strong evidence*:

Results of three recent studies **strongly suggest** that X and Y are....

Most studies of X and Y **clearly indicate the possibility** that X and Y are....

This type of evidence **has led most researchers to conclude** that X and Y....

Terms that researchers can use to indicate that the results of research offer moderate to weak evidence are shown in Example 5.6.2.

**Example 5.6.2**

*Examples of terminology (in bold) that can be used to indicate moderate to weak evidence*:

The results of a recent pilot study **suggest** that X and Y are....

To date, there is **only limited evidence** that X and Y are....

Although empirical evidence **is inconclusive**, X and Y seem to be....

Recent research **indicates** that X and Y....

The relationship between X and Y has been examined, with results **pointing toward**....

It may not be necessary to indicate the degree of confidence that should be accorded every finding discussed in a literature review. However, a literature review in which this is not done for any of the findings indicates that the writer lacks a full understanding of the fundamental limits of empirical research.

## ___ 7. Has the researcher avoided the overuse of direct quotations from the literature?

Very satisfactory  5  4  3  2  1  Very unsatisfactory  *or*  N/A  I/I

*Comment*: Direct quotations should be rarely used in literature reviews for two reasons. First, they often take up more journal space, which is very limited, than a paraphrase would take. Second, they often interrupt the flow of the text because of differences in writing styles of the reviewer and the author of the literature.

An occasional quotation may be used if it expresses an idea or concept that would lose its impact in a paraphrase. This may be the case with a quotation shown in Example 5.7.1, which appeared in the first paragraph of a research report on drug abuse and its association with loneliness.

**Example 5.7.1**[10]

*A direct quotation in a literature review (acceptable if done very sparingly)*:

Recent studies suggest that a large proportion of the population are frequently lonely (Rokach & Brock, 1997). Ornish (1998) stated at the very beginning of his book *Love & Survival*: "Our survival depends on the healing power of love, intimacy, and relationships. Physically. Emotionally. Spiritually. As individuals. As communities. As a culture. Perhaps even as a species." (p. 1.) Indeed, loneliness has been linked to depression, anxiety and....

**___ 8. Overall, is the literature review portion of the Introduction appropriate?**

Very satisfactory   5   4   3   2   1   Very unsatisfactory   *or*   N/A   I/I

*Comment*: Rate this evaluation question after considering your answers to the earlier ones in this chapter and any additional considerations and concerns you may have. Be prepared to explain your overall evaluation.

# Exercise for Chapter 5

**Part A**

*Directions*: Answer the following questions.

1. Do you agree that a long string of references to support a single point is usually inappropriate? (See Evaluation Question 1.) Instead, would you support the argument that citing a large number of references shows that there is great support for the point being made? Does a large number indicate that the researcher has conducted a thorough literature review?

---

[10] Orzeck, T., & Rokach, A. (2004). Men who abuse drugs and their experience of loneliness. *European Psychologist, 9*, 163–169.

2. Consider Statement A and Statement B below. They both contain the same citations. In your opinion, which statement is superior? Explain.

> **Statement A**: "The overall positive association between nonverbal decoding skills and workplace effectiveness has replicated with adults in a variety of settings (Campbell, Kagan, & Krathwohl, 1971; Costanzo & Philpott, 1986; Schag, Loo, & Levin, 1978; DiMatteo, Friedman, & Taranta, 1979; Tickle-Degnen, 1998; Halberstadt & Hall, 1980; Izard, 1971; Izard et al., 2001; Nowicki & Duke, 1994)."

> **Statement B**: "The overall positive association between nonverbal decoding skills and workplace effectiveness has replicated with adults in counseling settings (Campbell, Kagan, & Krathwohl, 1971; Costanzo & Philpott, 1986; Schag, Loo, & Levin, 1978) and medical settings (DiMatteo, Friedman, & Taranta, 1979; Tickle-Degnen, 1998) and with children in academic settings (Halberstadt & Hall, 1980; Izard, 1971; Izard et al., 2001; Nowicki & Duke, 1994)."[11]

3. Consider Statement C and Statement D below. Does the term "well established in the literature" in Statement D influence your interpretation of the statement? Explain.

> **Statement C**: "Parents and grandparents provide protective influence on pregnant and parenting adolescents' well-being (Apfel & Seitz, 1996; Wilson, 1986). However, far less attention has been paid to the role of siblings."

> **Statement D**: "Although the protective influence of parent and grandparent support on pregnant and parenting adolescents' well-being has been well established in the literature (Apfel & Seitz, 1996; Wilson, 1986), far less attention has been paid to the role of siblings."[12]

**Part B**

*Directions*: Read three research reports in academic journals on a topic of interest to you. Apply the evaluation questions in this chapter to the literature reviews in their Introductions, and select the one to which you gave the highest ratings. Bring it to class for discussion. Be prepared to discuss its specific strengths and weaknesses. Also, examine it to see if it has at least one example of each of the following. If so, mark the examples and be prepared to discuss them in class.

4. A positive, critical statement about literature being cited (e.g., In a well-designed study, Smith (2004) found....).

---

[11] Effenbein, H. A., & Ambady, N. (2002). Predicting workplace outcomes from the ability to eavesdrop on feelings. *Journal of Applied Psychology*, 87, 963–971.
[12] Gee, C. B., Nicholson, M. J., Osborne, L. N., & Rhodes, J. E. (2003). Support and strain in pregnant and parenting adolescents' sibling relationships. *Journal of Adolescent Research*, 18, 25–35.

5. A negative, critical statement about literature being cited (e.g., Because of the high attrition rate, it is difficult to interpret Smith's findings.).

6. An opinion expressed by the researcher that is explicitly introduced as such with terms such as "speculation" or "logical argument."

7. A statement about a theory (clearly identified as theory) with a research finding (clearly identified as a research finding) relating to the theory.

*Notes*:

# Chapter 6

# Evaluating Samples When Researchers Generalize

Immediately after the Introduction, which includes a literature review, most researchers insert the main heading of "Method." In the Method section, researchers almost always begin by describing the individuals they studied. This description is usually prefaced with one of these subheadings: "Subjects" or "Participants." [1]

A *population* is any group in which a researcher is ultimately interested. It might be large, such as all registered voters in Pennsylvania, or it might be small, such as all members of a local teachers' association. Researchers often study only *samples* (i.e., a subset of a population) for the sake of efficiency and then *generalize* their results to the population of interest. In other words, they infer that the data[2] they collected by studying samples are similar to the data they would have obtained by studying the entire population.

Because many researchers do not explicitly state whether they are attempting to generalize, you will often need to make a judgment on this matter in order to decide whether to apply the evaluation questions in this chapter to the research report you are evaluating. To make this decision, consider these questions:

Does the researcher *imply* that the results apply to some larger population?

Does the researcher discuss the implications of his or her research for a larger group of individuals than the one directly studied?

Note that the answers to these questions may be found anywhere in a research report, so you will need to read the entire report before answering them. If the answers are clearly "yes," you should apply the evaluation questions in this chapter to the article you have read. Note that the evaluation of samples when researchers are clearly *not* attempting to generalize to populations is considered in the next chapter.

## ___ 1. Was random sampling used?

Very satisfactory  5  4  3  2  1  Very unsatisfactory  *or*  N/A  I/I

---

[1] For most of the 1900s, the standard subheading was "Subjects." Near the end of the century, "Participants" became popular. The term *participant* indicates that the people being studied have consented to participate after being informed of the nature of the research project, its potential benefits, and its potential harm.

[2] Note that the term *data* is plural. Hence, it is correct to say, "the data are," and it is incorrect to say, "the data is."

*Comment*: Using random sampling (like drawing names out of a hat) yields an *unbiased* sample (i.e., a sample that does not systematically favor any particular type of individual or group in the selection process). If a sample is unbiased and large, researchers are likely to make sound generalizations. (Sample size will be discussed later in this chapter.)

The desirability of using random samples as the basis for making generalizations is so widely recognized among researchers that they are almost certain to mention its use if it was employed in selecting their samples. Example 6.1.1 shows three instances of how this has recently been expressed in published research.

### Example 6.1.1

*Brief description of the use of random sampling in three research articles*:

Surveys were sent to 600 psychologists who were randomly selected from a list of 872 licensed psychologists who were members of the Illinois Psychological Association.[3]

A random national sample composed of 681 licensed practicing psychologists who are members of the American Psychological Association's Division 20 (Adult Development and Aging) was surveyed regarding assessment and treatment of suicide risk in older adult patients and perception of risk factors for completed suicide among older adults.[4]

Participants were randomly sampled by household address from Colorado's general population....[5]

### ___ 2. If random sampling was used, was it stratified?

Very satisfactory   5   4   3   2   1   Very unsatisfactory   *or*   N/A   I/I

*Comment*: Researchers use *stratified random sampling* by drawing individuals separately at random from different strata (i.e., subgroups) within a population. For instance, suppose a researcher wants to survey licensed clinical psychologists in a large city. To stratify, he or she might divide the population into four subgroups: those who practice on the north side of town, those who practice on the east side, and so on. Then he or she could draw a fixed percentage at random from each side of town. The result will be a sample that is geographically representative. For instance, if 40% of the population practices on the west side, then 40% of the sample will be from the west side.

---

[3] Stevanovic, P., & Rupert, P. A. (2004). Career-sustaining behaviors, satisfactions, and stresses of professional psychologists. *Psychotherapy: Theory, Research, Practice, Training, 41*, 301–309.
[4] Brown, L. M., Bongar, B., & Cleary, K. M. (2004). A profile of psychologists' views of critical risk factors for completed suicide in older adults. *Professional Psychology: Research and Practice, 35*, 90–96.
[5] Plant, E. A., & Sachs-Ericsson, N. (2004). Racial and ethnic differences in depression: The roles of social support and meeting basic needs. *Journal of Consulting and Clinical Psychology, 72*, 41–52.

Stratifying will improve a sample only if the stratification variable (e.g., "geography") is related to the variables to be studied. For instance, if the researcher is planning to study how psychologists work with illicit substance abusers, stratifying on geography will improve the sample if the various areas of the city tend to have different types of drug problems, which may require different treatment modalities.

Note that *geography* is often an excellent variable on which to stratify because people tend to cluster geographically based on many variables that are important in the social and behavioral sciences. For example, they often cluster according to race/ethnicity, income/personal wealth, language preference, religion, and so on. Thus, a geographically representative sample is likely to be representative in terms of these other variables as well. Other common stratification variables are occupation, highest educational level attained, political affiliation, and age.

In Example 6.2.1, geography was used as a stratification variable. By stratifying, the researchers were able to obtain a representative sample of population sizes of Kentucky counties.

### Example 6.2.1[6]

*Description of the use of stratified random sampling*:

The data for our investigation came from a survey of 3,690 seventh-grade students from 65 middle schools in randomly selected counties in the state of Kentucky. Four strata were used: (1) counties with a minimum population of 150,000, (2) counties with population sizes between 40,000 and 150,000, (3) counties with population sizes between 15,000 and 40,000, and (4) counties with population sizes below 15,000.

If random sampling without stratification is used, the technique is called *simple random sampling*. In contrast, if stratification is used to form subgroups from which random samples are drawn, the technique is called *stratified random sampling*.

Despite the almost universal acceptance that an unbiased sample obtained through simple or stratified random sampling is highly desirable for making generalizations, the vast majority of research from which researchers want to make generalizations is based on studies in which nonrandom (biased) samples were used. There are three major reasons for this:

1. Even though a random selection of names has been drawn, the researcher may not be able to convince all those selected to participate in the research project. This problem is addressed in the next two evaluation questions.

2. Many researchers have limited resources: limited time, money, and assistance to conduct research. Often, they will reach out to individuals who are readily accessible or convenient to use as participants. For instance, college professors conduct-

---

[6] This example is loosely based on the work of Ousey, G. C., & Wilcox, P. (2005). Subcultural values and violent delinquency: A multilevel analysis in middle schools. *Youth Violence and Juvenile Justice*, *3*, 3–22.

ing research often find that the most convenient samples consist of students enrolled in their classes, which are not even random samples of students on their campuses.

3. For some populations, it is difficult to identify all members. If a researcher cannot do this, he or she obviously cannot draw a random sample of the entire population. Examples of populations of this type are the homeless in a large city, successful burglars (i.e., those who have never been caught), and illicit drug users.

Because so many researchers study nonrandom samples, it is unrealistic to count failures on the first two evaluation questions in this chapter as fatal flaws in research methodology. If journal editors routinely refused to publish research reports with this type of deficiency, there would be very little published research on many of the most important problems in the social and behavioral sciences. Thus, when researchers use nonrandom samples when attempting to generalize, the additional evaluation questions raised below should be applied in order to distinguish between studies from which it might be reasonable to make tentative, very cautious generalizations and those that are hopelessly flawed with respect to their sampling.

## ___ 3. If the randomness of a sample is impaired by the refusal to participate by some of those selected, is the rate of participation reasonably high?

Very satisfactory   5   4   3   2   1   Very unsatisfactory   *or*   N/A   I/I

*Comment*: Defining "reasonably high" is problematic. For example, a professional survey organization, with trained personnel and substantial resources, would be concerned if it had a response rate of less than 80% when conducting a national survey by phone or in person. On the other hand, researchers with limited resources using mailed questionnaires often are satisfied with a return rate as low as 50%, especially because rates of returns to mailed surveys are often notoriously poor. As a very rough rule-of-thumb, then, response rates of substantially less than 50% raise serious concerns about the generalizability of the findings.

The percentages mentioned in the previous paragraph should not be applied mechanically when evaluating research because exceptions may be made for cases in which participation in the research is burdensome, invasive, or raises sensitive issues—factors that might make it understandable to obtain a lower rate of participation. For instance, if a researcher needed to draw samples of blood from students on campus to estimate the incidence of a certain type of infection or needed to put a sample of students through a series of rigorous physical fitness tests that spanned several days for a study in sports psychology, you might judge a participation rate of substantially less than 50% to be reasonable in light of the particulars of the research, keeping in mind that any generalizations to populations would be highly tenuous.

When applying this evaluation question, it is appropriate to consider how much effort a researcher put into trying to obtain a high rate of participation. For instance, if a researcher contacted the individuals who were selected several times (for instance, by phone, by mail, or in person) and still had a response rate of less than 50%, you might reach the conclusion that this is the highest rate of return that might be expected for the researcher's particular research problem and population. In effect, you might judge that this is the best that can be done, keeping in mind that generalizations from such a sample are exceedingly risky because nonparticipants might be fundamentally different from those who agree to participate. Example 6.3.1 describes the extensive efforts made to obtain a sample of married couples in the general (not college) population. Note that despite their efforts, including an incentive of $20 to complete the questionnaires, the response rate was only 37%.

### Example 6.3.1[7]

*Extensive efforts to obtain a sample:*

A mailing list with a random sample of married persons in a large metropolitan area was obtained from a commercial mail-distribution source. A four-step mailing procedure was used to maximize the response rate (Sheskin, 1985). The first step involved sending a postcard to 350 married individuals (175 couples) informing them that they would receive a request for participation and a packet of questionnaires in the next week. There were 18 (10%) postcards that were not deliverable. The questionnaires were sent with instructions for each spouse to complete the questionnaires privately and return them separately to the researcher in the envelopes provided. A financial incentive of $20 was offered to couples who completed the questionnaires. Potential respondents who did not complete the questionnaires two weeks after they were mailed were sent a reminder postcard. If the questionnaires were not received within 4 weeks after they were mailed, a second set of materials was sent. Following this procedure, 116 (37%) questionnaires were returned, 6 of which were not usable.

___ **4. If the randomness of a sample is impaired by the refusal to participate by some of those selected, is there reason to believe that the participants and nonparticipants are similar on relevant variables?**

Very satisfactory  5  4  3  2  1  Very unsatisfactory  *or*  N/A  I/I

*Comment*: In some instances, researchers have information about those who do not participate, which allows for a comparison of nonparticipants with participants. For in-

---

[7] Fowers, B. J., Lyons, E., Montel, K. H., & Shaked, N. (2001). Positive illusions about marriage among married and single individuals. *Journal of Family Psychology*, *15*, 95–109.

stance, a researcher might note the zip codes on the envelopes in which returned questionnaires were posted. This might allow a researcher to determine whether those in affluent neighborhoods were more responsive than those in less affluent ones.[8]

In institutional settings such as schools, hospitals, and prisons, it is often possible to determine whether participants and nonparticipants differ in important respects. For instance, in a survey regarding political attitudes held by college students, participants might be asked for background information such as major, GPA, and age. These background characteristics are usually known for all students on the campus, allowing for a comparison of participants and the entire student body. If there are substantial differences, the results will need to be interpreted in light of them. For instance, if political science majors formed a larger percentage of the participants than exists in the whole student body, the researcher should be highly cautious in generalizing the results to all students.

In the evaluation of a new component for the Head Start program in rural areas of Oregon, only 56% agreed to participate. The researchers noted, however, the similarities of these participants with the general population in Example 6.4.1. This provides some assurance that those who chose to participate in the research were not substantially different from nonparticipants in terms of important background characteristics (i.e., demographics).

### Example 6.4.1[9]

*Comparison of a flawed sample with a larger group*:

Forty-five percent of children [were] living in families including both biological parents. Sixty percent of the children and families received public assistance. Eighty-three percent were Caucasian, and 13% were other ethnic groups, primarily Hispanic. These demographics are representative of the rural population in Oregon.

### ___ 5. If a sample from which a researcher wants to generalize was not selected at random, is it at least drawn from the target group for the generalization?

Very satisfactory   5   4   3   2   1   Very unsatisfactory   *or*   N/A   I/I

*Comment*: There are many instances in the published literature in which a researcher studied one type of participant (e.g., college freshmen) and used the data to make gen-

---

[8] If such a bias were detected, statistical adjustments might be made to correct for it by mathematically giving more weight to the respondents from the underrepresented zip codes.

[9] Kaminski, R. A., Stormshak, E. A., Good, R. H., III, & Goodman, M. R. (2002). Prevention of substance abuse with rural Head Start children and families: Results of Project STAR. *Psychology of Addictive Behaviors, 16*, S11–S26.

eralizations to an entirely different target group (e.g., public school students).[10] If a researcher does not have the wherewithal to at least tap into the target group of interest, it might be better if he or she left the research to others with resources and contacts that give them access to members of the target group.

There are also many instances in which the nonrandom sample is drawn from a *specialized subgroup* from the population to which the researcher wants to generalize. For example, in a campus survey of athletes' attitudes toward performance-enhancing drugs, members of only certain athletic teams may be available, calling into question the generalizability of the results to all athletes on the campus.

## ___ 6. If a sample from which a researcher wants to generalize was not selected at random, is it at least reasonably diverse?

Very satisfactory  5  4  3  2  1  Very unsatisfactory  *or*  N/A  I/I

*Comment*: Did a researcher generalize to all college students after studying only students attending a small religious college in which 99% of the students have the same ethnic/racial background? Did a researcher generalize to men and women regarding the relationship between exercise and health after studying only men attending a cardiac unit's exercise program? An answer of "yes" to these types of questions might cause you to give a low rating to this evaluation question.

Research in which researchers point out the diversity of their sample (even though they could not use random sampling) should be regarded more highly than research in which the researchers are silent on this issue. Consider Example 6.6.1, in which the researchers explicitly address the issue of diversity.

### Example 6.6.1[11]
*Discussion of the diversity of a nonrandom sample*:

The participants were not a representative sample of young British Jews. Nevertheless, the researchers selected them carefully to reflect a broad range of characteristics relevant to the British Jewish population, from secular to orthodox.... Five were Orthodox and fully involved with Jewish religious and social life on a daily basis. Ten were "middle of the road" with a moderate or low degree of religious involvement.

---

[10] In this context, it is interesting to note that the editor of the *Journal of Adolescent Research* pointed out that "Many articles currently published in journals on adolescence are based on American middle-class samples but draw conclusions about adolescents in general." (p. 5). Arnett, J. J. (2005). The vitality criterion: A new standard of publication for *Journal of Adolescent Research*. *Journal of Adolescent Research, 20*, 3–7.

[11] Sinclair, J., & Milner, D. (2005). On being Jewish: A qualitative study of identity among British Jews in emerging adulthood. *Journal of Adolescent Research, 20*, 91–117.

When a researcher wants to generalize to a larger population in the absence of random sampling, also consider whether a researcher sought participants from several sources, which increases the odds of diversity. For instance, much educational research is conducted in single schools. In Example 6.6.2, the researchers used participants from 19 different schools.

### Example 6.6.2[12]

*Diversity sought by seeking participants from more than one source*:

Children from 19 different schools in a mid-sized southern city in the United States were studied....

## ___ 7. If a sample from which a researcher wants to generalize was not selected at random, does the researcher explicitly discuss this limitation?

Very satisfactory  5  4  3  2  1  Very unsatisfactory  *or*  N/A  I/I

*Comment*: While researchers may discuss the limitations of their methodology (including sampling) in any part of their reports, many explicitly discuss limitations in the Discussion section at the end of their reports. Example 6.7.1 appeared near the end of a research report.

### Example 6.7.1[13]

*Statement of a limitation in sampling*:

The limited number and geographic location (rural eastern North Carolina) of the churches in this study may not be generalizable to other types of churches, other population groups, or other geographic areas.

Example 6.7.2 is an acknowledgment of a sampling limitation that appeared as the last sentence in a research report.

### Example 6.7.2[14]

*Statement of a limitation in sampling*:

Finally, the fact that patients with a lifetime history of psychotic disorder, or alcohol or drug addiction, were not included in the study may have biased the

---

[12] Broussard, S. C., & Garrison, M. E. B. (2004). The relationship between classroom motivation and academic achievement in elementary-school-aged children. *Family and Consumer Sciences Research Journal*, *33*, 106–120.

[13] Campbell, M. K. et al. (2004). Improving multiple behaviors for colorectal cancer prevention among African American church members. *Health Psychology*, *23*, 492–502.

[14] Chioqueta, A. P., & Stiles, T. C. (2004). Suicide risk in patients with somatization disorder. *Crisis: The Journal of Crisis Intervention and Suicide*, *25*, 3–7.

sample, limiting the generalizability of the findings. The results should be treated with caution, and replication, preferably including a larger sample size, is recommended.

Such acknowledgments of limitations do not improve researchers' ability to generalize. However, they do perform two important functions: (a) they serve as warnings to naïve readers regarding the problem of generalizing, and (b) they reassure all readers that the researchers are aware of a serious flaw in their methodology—a sign of the researchers' overall competence.

## ___ 8. Has the author described relevant demographics of the sample?

Very satisfactory   5   4   3   2   1   Very unsatisfactory   *or*   N/A   I/I

*Comment*: A researcher should describe the relevant demographics (i.e., background characteristics). For instance, when studying registered nurses' attitudes toward assisted suicide, it would be relevant to know their religious affiliations. For studying consumers' preferences, it would be helpful to know their economic status. Example 6.8.1 is from a study on hostility toward women, in which demographic information on participants' job status is especially important.

### Example 6.8.1[15]

*Description of relevant demographics*:

Participants ranged in age from 21 to 78 years ($M = 41.04$), and most were European American/White (89.1%), married (68.2%), employed full time (93.4%), and had at least some college or a college degree (75.2%). They had worked in this organization for an average of 5.34 years. Their job classifications were as follows: 15.2% were employed in management positions (i.e., units head, manager, or supervisor), 22.6% as attorneys, 15.9% as specialists (e.g., financial specialist, personnel specialist, budget analyst), 18% as secretaries, and 28.3% as administrative support staff (e.g., library technician, mailroom clerk).

In addition to demographics that are directly relevant to the variables being studied, it usually is desirable to give an overall demographic profile, including variables such as age, gender, race/ethnicity, and highest level of education. This is especially important when a nonrandom sample of convenience has been used because readers will want to visualize the particular participants who were part of such a sample.

---

[15] Miner-Rubino, K., & Cortina, L. M. (2004). Working in a context of hostility toward women: Implications for employees' well-being. *Journal of Occupational Health Psychology, 9*, 107–122.

## ____ 9. Is the overall size of the sample adequate?

Very satisfactory   5   4   3   2   1   Very unsatisfactory   *or*   N/A   I/I

*Comment*: Students who are new to research methods are sometimes surprised to learn that there often is no simple answer to the question of how large a sample should be. First, it depends in part on how much error a researcher is willing to tolerate. For public opinion polls, a stratified random sample of 1,500 drawn at random produces a margin of error of about one to three percentage points. A sample size of 400 produces a margin of error of about four to six percentage points.[16] If a researcher is trying to predict the outcome of a close election, clearly a sample size of 400 would be inadequate.[17]

Responding to a public opinion poll usually takes little time and may be of interest to many participants. Other types of studies, however, may be of less interest to potential participants and/or may require extensive effort on the part of participants. In addition, certain data collection methods (such as individual interviews) may require expenditure of considerable resources by researchers. Under such circumstances, it may be unrealistic to expect a researcher to use large samples. Thus, you should ask whether the researchers used a reasonable number given the particular circumstances of their studies. Would it have been an unreasonable burden to use substantially more participants? Is the number of participants so low that there is little hope of making sound generalizations? Would you base an important decision on the results of the study given the number of participants used? Your subjective answers to these types of questions will guide you on this evaluation question.[18]

It is important to keep in mind that a large sample size does not compensate for a bias in sampling due to the failure to use random sampling; that is, using large numbers of unrepresentative participants does not get around the problem of their unrepresentativeness.

## ____ 10. Is the number of participants in each group sufficiently large?

Very satisfactory   5   4   3   2   1   Very unsatisfactory   *or*   N/A   I/I

*Comment*: Consider the hypothetical information in Example 6.10.1, where the numbers of participants in each subgroup are indicated by *n*, and the mean (average) scores are indicated by *m*.

---

[16] The exact size of the margin of error depends on whether the sample was stratified and other sampling issues that are beyond the scope of this book.

[17] With a sample of only 400 individuals, there would need to be an 8 to 12 percentage-point *difference* (twice the four- to six-point margin of error) between the two candidates to make a reliable prediction (i.e., statistically significant prediction).

[18] There are statistical methods for estimating optimum sample sizes under various assumptions. While these methods are beyond the scope of this book, note that they do not take into account the practical matters raised here.

### Example 6.10.1

*A sample in which some subgroups are very small*:

A random sample of 100 college freshmen was surveyed on its knowledge of alcoholism. The mean (*m*) scores out of a maximum of 25 were as follows: White ($m = 18.5$, $n = 78$), African American ($m = 20.1$, $n = 11$), Hispanic/Latino(a) ($m = 19.9$, $n = 9$), and Chinese American ($m = 17.9$, $n = 2$). Thus, for each of the four ethnic/racial groups, there was a reasonably high average knowledge of alcoholism.

Although the total number in the sample is 100 (a number that would be considered fairly low for most research purposes), the numbers of participants in the last three subgroups in Example 6.10.1 are so small that it would be highly inappropriate to generalize from them to their respective populations. The researcher should either obtain larger numbers of them or refrain from separately reporting on the individual subgroups. Notice that there is nothing wrong with indicating ethnic/racial backgrounds (such as the fact that there were two Chinese American participants) as part of the description of the demographics of the sample. Instead, the problem is that the number of individuals in some of the subgroups is too small to justify calculating a mean and making an inference about them. For instance, a mean of 17.9 for the Chinese Americans is meaningless because there are only two individuals in this subgroup.

## ___11. Has informed consent been obtained?

Very satisfactory  5  4  3  2  1  Very unsatisfactory  *or*  N/A  I/I

*Comment*: It is almost always a good idea to get written, informed consent from the participants in a study. Participants should be informed of the nature of the study and, at least in general terms, the nature of their involvement. They should also be informed of their right to withdraw from the study at any time without penalty. Typically, researchers report only very briefly on this matter, as illustrated in Example 6.11.1, which presents a statement similar to many found in research reports in academic journals. It is unrealistic to expect much more detail than shown here because, by convention, the discussion of this issue is typically brief.

### Example 6.11.1

*Brief description of informed consent*:

Students from the departmental subject pool volunteered to participate in this study for course credit. Prior to participating in the study, students were given an informed consent form that had been approved by the university's institutional review board. The form described the experiment as "a study of social interactions between male and female students" and informed them that if they consented, they were free to withdraw from the study at any time without penalty.

There will be times when you judge that the study is so innocuous that informed consent might not be needed. A good example is an observational study in which individuals are observed in public places, such as a public park or shopping mall, while the observers are in plain view. Because public behaviors are being observed by researchers in such instances, privacy would not normally be expected, and informed consent may not be required.

## ___ 12. Overall, is the sample appropriate for generalizing?

Very satisfactory   5   4   3   2   1   Very unsatisfactory   *or*   N/A   I/I

*Comment*: Rate this evaluation question after considering your answers to the earlier ones in this chapter and any additional considerations and concerns you may have. Be prepared to discuss your response to this evaluation question.

# Concluding Comment

Although a primary goal of much research in all the sciences is to make sound generalizations from samples to populations, researchers in the social and behavioral sciences face special problems regarding access to and cooperation from samples of humans. Unlike other published lists of criteria for evaluating samples, this chapter urges you to be pragmatic when making these evaluations. A researcher may have some relatively serious flaws in sampling, yet you may conclude that he or she did a reasonable job under the circumstances he or she faced. However, this does not preclude the need to be exceedingly cautious in making generalizations from studies with weak samples. Confidence in certain generalizations based on weak samples can be increased, however, if various researchers with different patterns of weaknesses in their sampling methods arrive at similar conclusions when studying the same problems.

In the next chapter, the evaluation of samples when researchers do *not* attempt to generalize is considered.

# Exercise for Chapter 6

## Part A

*Directions*: Answer the following questions.

1. Suppose a researcher conducted a survey on a college campus by interviewing students that she/he approached while they were having dinner in the campus cafeteria one evening. In your opinion, is this a "random sample" of all students enrolled in the college? Even if you think it is not random, is it a reasonably good way to sample? Explain.

2. Briefly explain why *geography* is often an excellent variable on which to stratify when sampling.

3. According to this chapter, the vast majority of research is based on biased samples. Cite one reason that is given in this chapter for this circumstance.

4. If extensive efforts have been made to increase the rate of participation, and yet the response rate is low, how would you be willing to give the report a reasonably high rating for sampling? Explain.

5. Is it important to know whether participants and nonparticipants are similar on relevant variables? Explain.

6. Does the use of a large sample compensate for a bias in sampling? Explain.

## Part B

*Directions*: Locate several research reports in academic journals in which the researchers are concerned with generalizing from a sample to a population and apply the evaluation questions in this chapter. Select the one to which you gave the highest overall rating and bring it to class for discussion. Be prepared to discuss the strengths and weaknesses of the sampling method used.

*Notes*:

# Chapter 7

# Evaluating Samples When Researchers Do *Not* Generalize

As you know from the previous chapter, researchers often study samples in order to make inferences about the populations from which the samples were drawn. This process is known as generalizing.

Not all research is aimed at generalizing. Here are the major reasons why:

1. Researchers often conduct *pilot studies*. These are designed to determine the feasibility of methods for studying specific research problems. For instance, a novice researcher who wants to conduct an interview study of the social dynamics of safe-sex practices among high school students might conduct a pilot study to determine, among other things, how much cooperation can be obtained from school personnel for such a study, what percentage of the parents give permission for their children to participate in interviews on this topic, whether students have difficulty understanding the interview questions and whether they are embarrassed by them, the optimum length of the interviews, and so on. After the research techniques are refined in a pilot study with a sample of convenience, a more definitive study with a more appropriate sample for generalizing might be conducted. Note that it is not uncommon for journals to publish reports of pilot studies, especially if they yield interesting results and point to promising directions for future research. Also, note that while many researchers will explicitly identify their pilot studies as such (by using the term "pilot study"), at other times you will need to infer that a study is a pilot study from statements such as "The findings from this preliminary investigation suggest that...."[1]

2. Some researchers focus on *developing and testing theories*. A theory is a proposition or set of propositions that provides a cohesive explanation of the underlying dynamics of certain aspects of behavior. For example, self-verification theory indicates that people attempt to maintain stable self-concepts. Based on this theory, we can make a number of predictions. For instance, if the theory is correct, we might predict that people with poor self-concepts will seek out negative social reinforcement (e.g., seek out people who give them negative feedback about themselves) while avoiding or rejecting positive reinforcement. They do not do this because they enjoy negative reinforcement. Instead, according to the theory, it is an attempt to validate their perceptions of them-

---

[1] Falsetti, S., Resnick, H. S., & Davis, J. (2005). Multiple channel exposure therapy: Combining cognitive-behavioral therapies for the treatment of posttraumatic stress disorder with panic attacks. *Behavior Modification, 29*, 70–94.

selves.[2] Such predictions can be tested with empirical research, which sheds light on the validity of a theory as well as data that may be used to further develop and refine it.

In addition to testing whether the predictions made on the basis of a theory are supported by data, researchers conduct studies to determine under what circumstances the elements of a theory hold up (e.g., in intimate relationships only? with mildly as well as severely depressed patients?). One researcher might test one aspect of the theory with a convenience sample of adolescent boys who are being treated for depression, another might test a different aspect with a convenience sample of high-achieving women, and so on. Note that they are focusing on the theory as an evolving concept rather than as a static explanation that needs to be tested with a random sample for generalization to a population. These studies may be viewed as *developmental tests* of a theory. For *preliminary* developmental work of this type, rigorous and expensive sampling from large populations usually is not justified.

3. Some researchers prefer to study a *purposive sample* rather than a random one. A purposive sample is one in which a researcher has a special interest because the individuals in a sample have characteristics that make them especially rich sources of information. For example, an anthropologist who is interested in studying tribal religious practices might purposively select a tribe that has remained isolated and, hence, may have been less influenced by outside religions than other tribes that are less isolated. Note that the tribe is not selected at random but is selected deliberately (i.e., purposively). The use of purposive samples is a tradition in *qualitative* research. (If you have not done so already, see Appendix A for a brief overview of the differences between qualitative and quantitative research.)

4. Some researchers study entire populations—not samples. This is especially true in institutional settings such as schools where all the seniors in a school district (the population) might be tested. Nevertheless, when researchers write research reports on population studies, they should describe their populations in some detail.

### ___ 1. Has the researcher described the sample/population in sufficient detail?

Very satisfactory   5   4   3   2   1   Very unsatisfactory   *or*   N/A   I/I

*Comment*: As you know from the previous chapter, researchers should describe relevant demographics (i.e., background characteristics) of their participants when conducting studies in which they are generalizing from a sample to a population. This is also true when researchers are not attempting to generalize.

---

[2] For more information on this theory and its potential application to a particular behavioral issue, see Goodyear, R. K., Newcomb, M. D., & Locke. T. F. (2002). Pregnant Latina teenagers: Psychosocial and developmental determinants of how they select and perceive the men who father their children. *Journal of Counseling Psychology, 49*, 187–201.

Example 7.1.1 shows a description of demographics from a qualitative research report in which the researchers are seeking in-depth information about a group of women living in a shelter because of domestic violence. The description of the demographics helps consumers of research "see" the participants, which makes the results of the study more meaningful.

### Example 7.1.1[3]
*Detailed description of the demographics of participants*:

Ten participants were recruited from the local domestic violence shelter. They ranged in age from 20 to 47 years ($M = 35.4$, $SD = 7.5$). All 10 participants were women. Of the participants, 5 (50%) were Native American, 4 (40%) were European American, and 1 (10%) was Latina. Two (20%) participants were married, 2 (20%) were divorced, 2 (20%) were single, and 4 (40%) were separated from their spouses. Nine of the 10 (90%) participants had children, and the children's ages ranged from under 1 year to over 27 years. Educational levels included 5 (50%) participants who had taken some college or technical courses, 2 (20%) participants with a high school diploma or general equivalency diploma (GED), 1 participant (10%) with a 10th-grade education, 1 participant (10%) with a technical school degree, and 1 participant (10%) who was a doctoral candidate. Four participants were unemployed, 2 worked as secretaries, 1 worked as a waitress, 1 worked as a housekeeper, 1 worked in a local retail store, and 1 worked in a factory. Each participant listed a series of short-term, low-pay positions such as convenience store clerk.

### ____ 2. For a pilot study or developmental test of a theory, has the researcher used a sample with relevant demographics?

Very satisfactory  5  4  3  2  1  Very unsatisfactory  *or*  N/A  I/I

*Comment*: Studies that often fail on this evaluation question are those in which college students are used as participants (for convenience in sampling). For example, some researchers have stretched the limits of credulity by conducting studies in which college students are asked to respond to questions that are unrelated to their life experiences, such as asking unmarried, childless college women what disciplinary measures they would take if they discovered that their hypothetical teenage sons were using illicit drugs. Obviously, this might yield little relevant information even in a pilot study because of the mismatch between those of interest to the researcher and those who actually participated.

---

[3] Wettersten, K. B. et al. (2004). Freedom through self-sufficiency: A qualitative examination of the impact of domestic violence on the working lives of women in shelter. *Journal of Counseling Psychology, 51*, 447–462.

Less extreme examples are frequently found in published research literature. For instance, using college students in tests of learning theories when the theories were constructed to explain the learning behavior of children would be inappropriate. When applying this evaluation question to such studies, make some allowance for minor "misfits" between the sample used in a pilot study (or developmental test of a theory) and the population of ultimate interest. Keep in mind that pilot studies are not designed to provide definitive data—only preliminary information that will assist in refining future research.

## ___ 3. Even if the purpose is not to generalize to a population, has the researcher used a sample of adequate size?

Very satisfactory  5  4  3  2  1  Very unsatisfactory  *or*  N/A  I/I

*Comment*: Very preliminary studies might be conducted using exceedingly small samples. While such studies might be useful to the researcher who is testing out his or her methodology, the results frequently are not publishable. Because there are no scientific standards for what constitutes a reasonable sample size for a pilot study to be publishable, you will need to make subjective judgments when answering this evaluation question. Likewise, there are no standards for sample sizes for developmental tests of theory.

For purposive samples, which are common in qualitative research, the sample size may be determined by the availability of participants who fit the sampling profile for the purposive sample. For instance, to study the career paths of highly achieving women in education, a researcher might decide to use female directors of statewide education agencies. If there are only a handful of such women, the sample will necessarily be limited to that number. On the other hand, when there are many potential participants who meet the standards for a purposive sample, a researcher might continue contacting additional participants until the point of "saturation," that is, the point at which additional participants are adding little new information to the picture that is emerging from the data they are collecting. In other words, "saturation" occurs when new participants are revealing the same types of information as those who have already participated. Example 7.3.1 illustrates how this was described in the report of a qualitative study. Note the use of the term "data saturation" in the last sentence, which has been italicized to draw your attention to it. Using the criterion of data saturation sometimes results in the use of small samples.

**Example 7.3.1**[4]

*A statement using "data saturation" to justify the use of a small purposive sample in a qualitative study (italics added for emphasis)*:

Seven African American men who attended a western university were interviewed for this study. As a White man, I was unsure if African American men would have an interview with me without any prior personal contact. To address this, I was personally "vouched for" by someone the participants knew. Participants were also recruited through snowball sampling, the process of participants referring others to the researcher (Patton, 1990). Because of the depth and duration of the interviews in the present study (an average of 90 min), 7 interviewees afforded *data saturation*, the point when new data become redundant (Bogdan & Biklen, 1992).

Note that those who conduct qualitative research often have extended contact with their participants as a result of using techniques such as in-depth personal interviews or prolonged observational periods. With limited resources, their samples might necessarily be small. On the other hand, quantitative researchers often have more limited contact by using techniques such as written tests or questionnaires, which can be administered to many participants at little cost. As a result, you usually should expect quantitative researchers to use larger samples than qualitative researchers.

## ___ 4. If a purposive sample has been used, has the researcher indicated the basis for selecting individuals to include?

Very satisfactory   5   4   3   2   1   Very unsatisfactory   *or*   N/A   I/I

*Comment*: Even when researchers do not plan to generalize to a population, they should indicate the basis or criteria for the selection of their samples. Example 7.4.1 is taken from a qualitative study on gender differences in stress among professional managers. Notice that the researchers did not simply rely on managers they happened to know to serve as participants. Instead, they carefully selected a purposive sample of managers.

**Example 7.4.1**[5]

*A description of the criteria for selecting a purposive sample for a qualitative study*:

Participants were selected based on purposive criterion sampling from a list, purchased by the research team, that consisted of professionals who had mana-

---

[4] Diemer, M. A. (2002). Constructions of provider role identity among African American men: An exploratory study. *Cultural Diversity and Ethnic Minority Psychology, 8*, 30–40.

[5] Iwasaki, Y., MacKay, K. J., & Ristock, J. (2004). Gender-based analyses of stress among professional managers: An exploratory qualitative study. *International Journal of Stress Management, 11*, 56–79.

gerial positions in business, governmental, or nongovernmental organizations in a western Canadian city. The criteria for participation included the following: (a) individuals were responsible for making decisions that affected the direction of their business or organization on a regular basis and (b) individuals had to score 3, 4, or 5 on at least three of four questions that asked about level of stress in their work, family, personal life, and overall life situations using a 5-point scale (1 = *not stressful at all* to 5 = *extremely stressful*). The first criterion verified that each individual held a managerial position, whereas the second criterion ensured that the participant generally felt stressed in his or her life. A research assistant randomly called listings from the database to describe the purpose of the study, make sure these individuals met the criteria for being participants, explain tasks of each participant, and find out whether they were interested in being involved in the study. Attention was also paid to ensuring that both women and men were recruited to participate.

Note that even if a researcher calls his or her sample "purposive," usually it should be regarded as merely a sample of convenience unless the specific basis for selection is described.

### ___ 5. If a population has been studied, has it been clearly identified and described?

Very satisfactory  5  4  3  2  1  Very unsatisfactory  *or*  N/A  I/I

*Comment*: Researchers who conduct population studies often disguise the true identity of their populations (for ethical and legal reasons), especially if the results reflect negatively on the population. Nevertheless, information should be given that helps the reader visualize the population, as illustrated in Example 7.5.1. Notice that the specific city is not mentioned, which helps protect the identity of the participants. Also, note that "all social workers in a small city in the southeast" constitutes the population.

### Example 7.5.1
*Description of a population that was studied*:

All social workers in a small city in the southeast were interviewed. All were college graduates, with 11% holding master's degrees while the rest had bachelor's degrees. The average age (median) was 39.4. The self-reported ethnicity/racial groups were White (62%), African American (30%), and "decline to state" (8%). The average salary adjusted for education and years on the job ($41,200) was slightly above the regional average.

With information such as that provided in the example, readers can make educated judgments as to whether the results are likely to apply to other populations of social workers.

## ___ 6. Has informed consent been obtained?

Very satisfactory  5  4  3  2  1  Very unsatisfactory  *or*  N/A  I/I

*Comment*: This evaluation question was raised in the previous chapter on evaluating samples when researchers generalize. (See Evaluation Question 11 in Chapter 6.) It is being raised again in this chapter because it is an important question that applies whether or not researchers are attempting to generalize.

## ___ 7. Overall, is the description of the sample adequate?

Very satisfactory  5  4  3  2  1  Very unsatisfactory  *or*  N/A  I/I

*Comment*: Rate this evaluation question after considering your answers to the earlier ones in this chapter and any additional considerations and concerns you may have.

# Exercise for Chapter 7

**Part A**

*Directions*: Answer the following questions.

1. Very briefly explain in your own words how theory development might impact the selection of a sample.

2. The use of *purposive* samples is a tradition in which type of research?
   A. qualitative    B. quantitative

3. Suppose you were evaluating a research report on college students' voting behavior. What are some demographics that you think should be described for such a study?

4. Very briefly describe in your own words the meaning of *data saturation*. Is this concept more closely affiliated with quantitative or qualitative research?

5. Which of the evaluation questions was regarded as so important that it is posed in both Chapter 6 and this chapter?

## Part B

*Directions*: Locate three research reports of interest to you in academic journals in which the researchers are not directly concerned with generalizing from a sample to a population, and apply the evaluation questions in this chapter. Note that many qualitative researchers deliberately do *not* concern themselves with generalizability, so such reports are likely to contain descriptions that will be useful for this part of the exercise. Select the one to which you gave the highest overall rating and bring it to class for discussion. Be prepared to discuss its strengths and weaknesses.

# Chapter 8

# Evaluating Instrumentation

Immediately after describing the sample or population they studied, researchers typically describe their *instruments*. An instrument is a technical term for any tool or method for measuring a trait or characteristic. The description of instruments usually is identified with the subheading *Instrumentation*.[1]

Often, researchers use previously published instruments developed by others. These are easy to spot because their titles will be capitalized and references for them will usually be given. About equally as often, researchers use instruments that they devise specifically for their particular research purposes. As a general rule, researchers should provide more information about such newly developed measures than on previously published instruments that have been described in detail in other publications, such as test manuals and other research reports.

While you would need to take several sequential courses in measurement to become an expert, you will be able to make preliminary evaluations of researchers' measurement procedures by applying the evaluation questions discussed below. Of course, your evaluations will be more definitive if you have first taken a measurement course or studied the chapter(s) on measurement in your research methods textbook.

## ____ 1. Have the actual items and questions (or at least a sample of them) been provided?

Very satisfactory  5  4  3  2  1  Very unsatisfactory  *or*  N/A  I/I

*Comment*: Providing sample items and questions is highly desirable because they help to operationalize what was measured. Note that researchers *operationalize* when they specify the physical properties of the concepts on which they are reporting.

In Example 8.1.1, the researcher provided a sample item for each of the three subscales on the Color-Blind Racial Attitudes Scale (CoBRAS). The provision of these items helps consumers of research understand how the variable was measured.

---

[1] As you know from Chapter 1, *observation* is a broad term that encompasses all forms of *measurement*. The term *instrumentation* refers to the materials and tests that are used to make the observations or obtain the measurements. "Sample" and "Instrumentation" are subheadings under the main heading "Method" in a research report.

**Example 8.1.1**[2]

*Portion of a description of a scale with a sample item for each subscale:*

The CoBRAS is a 20-item measure of contemporary racial attitudes. The scale measures participants' lack of awareness or denial of racism in the United States. Items are assessed on a Likert scale ranging from 1 (*strongly agree*) to 6 (*strongly disagree*). The total scale comprises three subscales. The first measures unawareness of White racial privilege and includes seven items (e.g., "everyone who works hard, no matter what race they are, has an equal chance to become rich"). The second subscale measures unawareness of institutional racism, with seven items (e.g., "social policies, such as affirmative action, discriminate unfairly against White people"). The third 6-item subscale assesses unawareness of blatant racial issues (e.g., "racial problems in the U.S. are rare, isolated situations"). Item scores are added to obtain subscale scores and a total score. A higher score means higher levels of unawareness or denial of racism.

In Example 8.1.2, the researchers provide the wording of an interview question that was posed to adults in a national survey. Notice that the term "regular household bills" is defined by giving examples. This was done to ensure that the respondents all had a common understanding of the term. Also, note that by being given the actual words used in the questions, readers of the research can evaluate whether the vocabulary level is appropriate for the participants (in this case, the general adult population) as well as whether the choices are comprehensive.

**Example 8.1.2**[3]

*Sample interview question:*

In your household, who makes sure that regular household bills are paid? I mean things like the bills for gas, electricity, [and] telephone.

1__Mainly you

2__Mainly your husband/wife/partner

3__Jointly with your husband/wife/partner

4__Or someone else? [WRITE IN]

Many achievement tests have items that vary in difficulty. When this is the case, including sample items that show the range of difficulty is desirable. The researchers who wrote Example 8.1.3 did this.

---

[2] Gushue, G. V. (2004). Race, color-blind racial attitudes, and judgments about mental health: A shifting standards perspective. *Journal of Counseling Psychology, 51,* 398–407.

[3] Zipp, J. F., & Toth, J. (2002). She said, he said, they said: The impact of spousal presence in survey research. *Public Opinion Quarterly, 66,* 177–208.

**Example 8.1.3**[4]

*Sample achievement items that show their range of difficulty:*

This task [mental computation of word problems] was taken from the arithmetic subtest of the WISC-III (Wechsler, 1991). Each word problem was orally presented and was solved without paper or pencil. Questions ranged from simple addition (e.g., If I cut an apple in half, how many pieces will I have?) to more complex calculations (e.g., If three children buy tickets to the show for $6.00 each, how much change do they get back from $20.00?).

Keep in mind that many instruments are copyrighted, and their copyright holders might insist on keeping the actual items secure from public exposure. Obviously, a researcher should not be faulted for failing to provide samples when this is the case.

## ___ 2. Are any specialized response formats, settings, and/or restrictions described in detail?

Very satisfactory  5  4  3  2  1  Very unsatisfactory  *or*  N/A  I/I

*Comment*: If a researcher has provided samples of the actual items, questions, or directions, as in Examples 8.1.1, 8.1.2, and 8.1.3, the response format may already be clear.

Examples of settings that should be mentioned are the place where the measures were used (such as in the participants' homes) and whether other individuals were present (such as whether parents were present while their children were interviewed).

Examples of restrictions that should be mentioned are time limits and tools that participants are permitted (or are not permitted) to use, such as not allowing the use of calculators while taking a mathematics test.

Qualitative researchers also should provide details on how they collected their information, even if they use loosely structured instruments such as unstructured interviews and informal observations. This is illustrated in Example 8.2.1 in which the setting, the length of the interviews, who was present, and other details are given for a qualitative study of children's understanding of historical change. Note that some of the photographs used during the interviews were reproduced in the journal article.

**Example 8.2.1**[5]

*Description of data collection in a qualitative study:*

[I conducted] open-ended, semistructured interviews with 121 students, aged 6–

---

[4] Swanson, H. L., & Beebe-Frankenberger, M. (2004). The relationship between working memory and mathematical problem solving in children at risk and not at risk for serious math difficulties. *Journal of Educational Psychology, 96*, 471–491.

[5] Barton, K. C. (2001). A sociocultural perspective on children's understanding of historical change: Comparative findings from Northern Ireland and the United States. *American Educational Research Journal, 38*, 881–913.

12 years, during a total of 60 interviews at the four schools. (Most students were interviewed in pairs.) In each interview, I showed students pictures from the past, asked them to arrange them in chronological order, to explain the reasons for their placements, and to estimate the approximate time period of each. I followed this task with more general questions about history. These included asking what aspects of life had changed over time and why, how people know how life was different in the past, why history is important, and where students had learned about the past. I frequently probed their answers or asked additional questions to follow up on issues that arose during the interviews.

## ___ 3. When appropriate, are multiple methods used to collect data/information on each variable?

Very satisfactory  5  *4*  3  2  1  Very unsatisfactory  *or*  N/A  I/I

*Comment*: As you know from Chapter 1, it is safe to assume that all methods of observation (e.g., testing, interviewing, making observations) are flawed. Thus, the results of a study are usually more conclusive if more than one method for collecting the data has been used.

In quantitative research, researchers emphasize developing objective measures that meet high statistical standards for reliability and validity, which are discussed later in this chapter. When researchers use these highly developed measures, they often do not believe that it is important to use multiple measures. For instance, they might use a well-established multiple-choice reading comprehension test that was extensively investigated (as to its validity and reliability) prior to publication of the test. A quantitative researcher would be *unlikely* to supplement such highly developed measures with other measures such as teachers' ratings of students' reading comprehension or some other measurement technique such as having each child read aloud and discuss what they learned from reading. Thus, as it turns out, it is not traditional to use multiple measures in quantitative research.

In qualitative research, researchers are more likely to use multiple measures of a single phenomenon for several reasons.[6] First, qualitative researchers strive to conduct research that is intensive and yields highly detailed results (often in the form of themes supported by verbal descriptions—as opposed to numbers). The use of multiple measures helps qualitative researchers probe more intensively from different points of view. In addition, qualitative researchers tend to view their research as exploratory. In advance of conducting exploratory research, it is difficult to know which type of measure for a particular variable is likely to be most useful. Finally, qualitative researchers see the use of multiple measures as a way to check the validity of their results. In other words, if different measures of the same phenomenon yield highly con-

---

[6] Qualitative researchers often use the term "triangulation of data sources" when they use multiple measures for the same purpose.

sistent results, the validity of the instrumentation (including the interpretation of the data) might be more highly regarded as being valid than if only one data source was used.

In Example 8.2.1 above, the researcher describes how he conducted the interviews in a qualitative study. In addition, he conducted classroom observations in the same study, as described in Example 8.3.1. Thus, he used multiple measures to study the traits of interest in his research.

### Example 8.3.1[7]

*Information on classroom observations in addition to interviews*:

I observed most of the history lessons taught in the integrated primary school during approximately a 3-month period from September to December, for a total of 38 observations lasting about 40–50 minutes each. Combining interviews with classroom observations had the advantage of allowing comparisons of students' responses to what they had learned in class, as well as providing the chance to ask questions about the content that arose in the course of instruction.

Sometimes, it is not realistic to expect researchers to use multiple measures of all variables. For instance, measurement of some variables is so straightforward that it would be poor use of a researcher's time to measure them in several ways. For example, most researchers would be very confident in the validity of asking second-grade students to perform the one-digit multiplication facts on a paper-and-pencil test. It would be needlessly redundant to ask the students to demonstrate their achievement a second time by having an interviewer ask the same students to answer the same multiplication facts.

### \_\_\_\_ 4. For published instruments, have sources where additional information can be obtained been cited?

Very satisfactory   5   4   3   2   1   Very unsatisfactory   *or*   N/A   I/I

*Comment*: Some instruments are "published" only in the sense that they were previously reproduced in full in journal articles. Such articles typically describe the development and statistical properties of the instruments. Other instruments are published by commercial publishers as separate publications (e.g., test booklets) that usually have accompanying manuals that describe technical information on the instruments. Researchers should provide references to sources of additional information on the published instruments they use in their research.

In Example 8.4.1, the researchers briefly describe the nature of one of the instruments they used followed by a statement that the validity and reliability of the in-

---

[7] Ibid.

strument have been established. It is important to note that they provide a reference (i.e., Pavot & Diener) where more information on the instrument's reliability and validity may be found.

### Example 8.4.1[8]

*Brief description of an instrument in which a reference for more information on reliability and validity is provided (bold added for emphasis)*:

The Satisfaction with Life Scale (Pavot & Diener, 1993) is a five-item, self-report scale that asks respondents to indicate their degree of agreement on a 7-point Likert scale (1 = *disagree*, 7 = *strongly agree*) to statements regarding life satisfaction. It has been used to measure the degree to which a person feels pleased with his or her current life situation. **It has well-demonstrated reliability and validity (Pavot & Diener, 1993).** The total score is the sum of the five items and is typically used to compare subjective well-being outcomes.

In Example 8.4.2, the researchers also briefly describe the nature of one of the instruments they used followed by a statement that it has "excellent psychometric properties." The term "psychometrics" originally meant "the science of psychological measurement" with an emphasis on reliability and validity. Currently, it refers to the science of measurement in all the social and behavioral sciences.

### Example 8.4.2[9]

*Brief description of an instrument in which a reference for more information on its psychometric properties is provided (bold added for emphasis)*:

The DMQ-R [Drinking Motives Questionnaire-Revised] (Cooper, 1994) is a 20-item self-report instrument that yields scores on four subscales representing the four motives for drinking (including CM and EM) identified in Cooper's (1994) model. Five items comprise each subscale, and the average of these items yields the subscale score. Respondents estimate how often they are motivated to drink for the reason specified in each item on a 5-point Likert scale. **It has been well established that the DMQ-R has excellent psychometric properties (Cooper, 1994; MacLean & Lecci, 2000).**

### ____ 5. When delving into sensitive matters, is there reason to believe that accurate data were obtained?

Very satisfactory   5   4   3   2   1   Very unsatisfactory   *or*   N/A   I/I

---

[8] Heinemann, A. W., Corrigan, J. D., & Moore, D. (2004). Case management for traumatic brain injury survivors with alcohol problems. *Rehabilitation Psychology, 49*, 156–166.

[9] Birch, C. D. ct al. (2004). Mood-induced increases in alcohol expectancy strength in internally motivated drinkers. *Psychology of Addictive Behaviors, 18*, 231–238.

*Comment*: Some issues are sensitive because they deal with illegal matters such as illicit substance use, gang violence, and so on. Others are sensitive because of societal taboos such as those regarding certain forms of sexual behavior. Still others may be sensitive because of idiosyncratic personal views on privacy. For instance, age and income are sensitive issues for many individuals; participants often decline to answer these questions or may not answer honestly. Thus, self-reports by participants may sometimes lack validity. The authors of Example 8.5.1 discuss the limitations of self-reports and how they might have affected the results of their research.

### Example 8.5.1[10]
*Discussion of limitations of self-reports in relation to a particular study*:

Our data are based exclusively on self-reported assessments of psychological distress, and, thus, our ability to draw conclusions is limited by the validity and reliability of this methodology. In general, self-report data are subject to threats to validity such as social desirability and response-style biases.[11] Thus, as suggested above, it may be that the veterans in the treatment groups were hesitant to acknowledge much change in the status of their distress as they may fear that to do so would impact their service connection or their identity associated with being a traumatized veteran.

A common technique for encouraging honest answers to sensitive questions is to collect the responses anonymously. For instance, participants may be asked to mail in questionnaires with the assurance that they are not coded in any way that would reveal their identity. In group settings, participants may also be assured that their responses are anonymous. However, if a group is small, such as a class of 20 students, some participants might be hesitant to be perfectly honest regarding highly sensitive matters because a small group does not provide much "cover" for hiding the identity of a participant who engages in illegal or taboo behaviors.

With techniques such as interviewing or direct physical observation, it is usually not possible to provide anonymity. The most a researcher might be able to do is assure *confidentiality*. Such an assurance is likely to work best if the participants already know and trust the interviewer (such as a school counselor) or if the researcher has spent enough time with the participants to develop rapport and trust. The latter is more likely to occur in qualitative research than quantitative research because qualitative researchers often spend substantial amounts of time in an effort to bond and interact with their participants.

---

[10] Bolton, E. E. et al. (2004). Evaluating a cognitive–behavioral group treatment program for veterans with posttraumatic stress disorder. *Psychological Services, 1,* 140–146.
[11] "Social desirability" refers to the tendency of some respondents to provide answers citing behaviors that are considered socially desirable. "Response-style bias" refers to the tendency of some respondents to respond in certain ways (such as tending to select the middle category on a scale) regardless of the content of the question.

**___ 6. Have steps been taken to keep the instrumentation from obtruding on and changing any overt behaviors that were observed?**

Very satisfactory  5  4  3  2  1  Very unsatisfactory  *or*  N/A  I/I

*Comment*: If participants know they are being directly observed, they may temporarily change their behavior. Clearly, this is likely to happen when studying highly sensitive behaviors, but it can also affect data collection on more ordinary matters. For instance, some students may show their best behavior if they come to class to find a newly installed video camera scanning the classroom (to gather research data); other students may show off by acting out in the presence of the camera.

One solution would be to make surreptitious observations, such as with a hidden video camera or by using a one-way mirror. In many circumstances, such techniques raise serious ethical and legal problems.

Another solution is to make the observational procedures a routine part of the research setting. For instance, if it is routine for a classroom to be visited frequently by outsiders (e.g., parents, school staff, and university observers), the presence of a researcher may be unlikely to obtrude on the behavior of the students.

**___ 7. If the collection and coding of observations is highly subjective, is there evidence that similar results would be obtained if another researcher used the same measurement techniques with the same group at the same time?**

Very satisfactory  5  4  3  2  1  Very unsatisfactory  *or*  N/A  I/I

*Comment*: Suppose a researcher observes groups of adolescent males interacting in various public settings, such as shopping malls, in order to collect data on aggressive behavior. Identifying some aggressive behaviors may require considerable subjectivity. If an adolescent puffs out his or her chest, is this a threatening behavior or merely a manifestation of a big sigh of relief? Is a scowl a sign of aggression or merely an expression of unhappiness? Answering such questions sometimes requires considerable subjectivity.

An important technique for addressing this issue is to have two or more independent observers make observations of the same participants at the same time. If the *rate of agreement* on the identification and classification of the behavior is reasonably high (say, 70% or more), a consumer of research will be assured that the resulting data are not idiosyncratic to one particular observer and his or her powers of observation and possible biases.

In Example 8.7.1, the researchers reported rates of agreement of 90% and 96%. Note that to achieve such high rates of agreement the researchers first trained the raters by having them rate the behavior with groups that were not part of the main study.

**Example 8.7.1**[12]

*Discussion of limitations of self-reports in relation to a particular study*:

Two independent raters first practiced the categorization of self-disclosure on five group sessions that were not part of this study and discussed each category until full agreement was reached. Next, each rater identified the "predominant behavior" (Hill & O'Brien, 1999)—that is, the speech turn that contained the disclosure—on which they reached agreement on 90%. Finally, each rater classified the participants into the three levels of self-disclosure. Interrater agreement was high (96%).

The rate of agreement is sometimes referred to as *interobserver reliability*. When the observations are reduced to scores for each participant (such as a total score for nonverbal aggressiveness), the scores based on two independent observers' observations can be expressed as an *interobserver reliability coefficient*. In reliability studies, these can range from 0.00 to 1.00, with coefficients of about 0.70 or higher indicating adequate interobserver reliability.[13]

___ **8. If an instrument is designed to measure a single unitary trait, does it have adequate internal consistency?**

Very satisfactory   5   4   3   2   1   Very unsatisfactory   *or*   N/A   I/I

*Comment*: A test of computational skills in mathematics at the primary grade levels measures a relatively homogenous trait. However, a mathematics battery that measures verbal problem-solving and mathematical reasoning in addition to computational skills measures a more heterogeneous trait. Likewise, a self-report measure of depression measures a much more homogenous trait than does a measure of overall mental health.

For instruments designed to measure homogenous traits, it is important to ask whether they are *internally consistent*, that is, to what extent are the items within the instrument consistent with each other in terms of what they measure? While it is beyond the scope of this book to explain how and why it works, a statistic known as Cronbach's alpha (whose symbol is $\alpha$) provides a statistical measure of internal consistency. As a special type of correlation coefficient, it ranges from 0.00 to 1.00, with values of about 0.70 or above indicating adequate internal consistency.[14] Values below

---

[12] Shechtman, Z., & Rybko, J. (2004). Attachment style and observed initial self-disclosure as explanatory variables of group functioning. *Group Dynamics: Theory, Research, and Practice, 8*, 207–220.

[13] Mathematically, these coefficients are the same as *correlation coefficients*, which are covered in all standard introductory statistics courses. You may know that correlation coefficients can range from −1.00 to 1.00, with a value of 0.00 indicating no relationship. In practice, however, negatives are not found in reliability studies. Values near 1.00 indicate a high rate of agreement.

[14] *Split-half reliability* also measures internal consistency, but Cronbach's alpha is widely considered a superior measure. Hence, split-half reliability is seldom reported.

this suggest that more than one trait is being measured by the instrument, which is undesirable when a researcher wants to measure only one homogenous trait. In example 8.8.1, the value of Cronbach's alpha is above the cutoff point of 0.70.

### Example 8.8.1[15]

*Statement regarding internal consistency using Cronbach's alpha*:

Parental discipline (Parental Attitudes toward Childrearing Scale, Easterbrooks & Goldberg, 1984), a 20-item measure…reflected mothers' self-reports of strictness of discipline practices and structure in child management ($M = 3.45$, $SD = .50$, Cronbach's alpha = .75).

Internal consistency usually is regarded as an issue only when an instrument is designed to measure a single homogenous trait *and* when the instrument yields scores (as opposed to instruments such as interviews when used to identify patterns that are described in words). If an instrument does not meet these two criteria, you should answer "not applicable" to this evaluation question.

## ___ 9. For stable traits, is there evidence of temporal stability?

Very satisfactory   5   4   3   2   1   Very unsatisfactory   *or*   N/A   I/I

*Comment*: Suppose a researcher wants to measure aptitude (i.e., potential) for learning algebra. Such an aptitude is widely regarded as being stable. In other words, it is unlikely to fluctuate much from one week or even one year to another without additional mathematics instruction. Hence, a test of such an aptitude should yield results that are stable across at least short periods of time. To put it more concretely, if a student's score on such a test administered this week indicates that he or she has very little aptitude for learning algebra, this test should yield a similar assessment if administered to the same student next week.

Although it is a little harder to see in the area of personality measurement, most measures of personality also should yield results that have temporal stability (i.e., are stable over time). For example, suppose a researcher wants to measure the deep-seated, long-term self-esteem of participants. While self-esteem may fluctuate modestly over even short periods of time, a researcher usually does *not* want a measure that is overly sensitive to such temporary fluctuations. Hence, he or she would want to use a measure that yields scores that are similar from one week or one month to another.

The most straightforward approach to assessing temporal stability is to administer the instrument to a group of participants twice at different points in time—typically

---

[15] Mowbray, C., Oyserman, D., Bybee, D., & MacFarlane, P. (2002). Parenting of mothers with a serious mental illness: Differential effects of diagnosis, clinical history, and other mental health variables. *Social Work Research, 26*, 225–240.

with a couple of weeks between administrations, although sometimes it is examined over a more extended period of time. The two sets of scores can be correlated, and if a coefficient (whose symbol is $r$) of about 0.70 or more (on a scale from 0.00 to 1.00) is obtained, there is evidence of temporal stability. This type of reliability is commonly known as *test-retest reliability*. As its name implies, this type of reliability is usually examined only when *tests* or scales that yield scores are used in research.

While temporal stability is an important issue, it usually is addressed in research reports mainly when researchers use previously published instruments that have been extensively studied. Unfortunately, researchers seldom examine temporal stability when using newly developed instruments in a particular study on which they are reporting because establishing temporal reliability would constitute a study in and of itself. However, there are exceptions. Example 8.9.1 illustrates how researchers describe how they established the test-retest reliability of their instrument. Note that they use the symbol $r$ and report a value well above the suggested cutoff point of 0.70.

### Example 8.9.1[16]

*Statement regarding temporal stability (test-retest reliability) established by the researchers*:

This inventory [designed to measure literacy] was piloted on a group of 50 students who did not attend any of the 10 schools in this study and were not considered part of this study. The test-retest reliability was $r = .82$.

In Example 8.9.2, the researchers report on the test-retest reliability coefficients that were reported earlier by other researchers (i.e., McNeilly et al.). Note that the reliabilities were reported separately for each of the four domains measured. All of them were above the suggested 0.70 cutoff point for acceptability.

### Example 8.9.2[17]

*Statement regarding temporal stability (test-retest reliability) established earlier and cited by the researchers*:

The PRS [Perceived Racism Scale] is a 32-item instrument that measures emotional reactions to racism [in four domains].... McNeilly et al. (1996) reported...test-retest reliability coefficients ranging from .71 to .80 for the four domains.

---

[16] Fisher, D., Lapp, D., & Flood, J. (2001). The effects of access to print through the use of community libraries on the reading performance of elementary students. *Reading Improvement, 38*, 175–182.

[17] Liang, C. T. H., Li, L. C., & Kim, B. S. K. (2004). The Asian American Racism-Related Stress Inventory: Development, factor analysis, reliability, and validity. *Journal of Counseling Psychology, 51*, 103–114.

## ___ 10. When appropriate, is there evidence of content validity?

Very satisfactory  5  4  3  2  1  Very unsatisfactory  *or*  N/A  I/I

*Comment*: An important issue in the evaluation of achievement tests is the extent to which the contents of the tests (i.e., the stimulus materials and skills) are suitable in light of the research purpose. For instance, if a researcher has used an achievement test to study the extent to which the second graders in a school district have achieved the skills expected of them at this grade level, an evaluator of the research will want to know whether the contents of the test are aligned with (or match) the contents of the second-grade curriculum.

While content validity is most closely associated with measurement of achievement, it also is sometimes used as a construct for evaluating other types of measures. For instance, in Example 8.10.1, the researchers revised a goal orientation scale and then had it assessed for content validity.

### Example 8.10.1[18]
*A personality scale subjected to content validation*:

Twenty items adapted from Button et al.'s (1996) goal orientation scale, two items adapted from Elliot and Church's (1997) achievement goal scale, and ten newly created items were used to develop an initial measure of dispositional goal orientation. The item pool was reviewed by a panel of PhD students for…content validity.

## ___ 11. When appropriate, is there evidence of empirical validity?

Very satisfactory  5  4  3  2  1  Very unsatisfactory  *or*  N/A  I/I

*Comment*: Empirical validity refers to validity established by collecting data using the instrument in order to determine the extent to which the data "make sense." For instance, a depression scale might be empirically validated by administering it to an institutionalized, clinically depressed group of adult patients as well as to a random sample of adult patients visiting family physicians for annual checkups. We would expect that the scores of the two groups will differ substantially in a predicted direction (i.e., the institutionalized sample should have higher depression scores). If not, the validity of the scale would be quite questionable.

Sometimes, the empirical validity of a test is expressed with a correlation coefficient. For example, a test maker might correlate scores on the College Board's SATs with freshman grades in college. A correlation of .40 or more might be interpreted as indicating the test has validity as a modest predictor of college grades.

---

[18] Zweig, D., & Webster, J. (2004). Validation of a multidimensional measure of goal orientation. *Canadian Journal of Behavioural Science, 36*, 232–243.

Empirical validity comes in many forms, and a full exploration of it would require a book of its own. Some key terms that suggest that empirical validity has been explored are *predictive validity*, *concurrent validity*, *criterion-related validity*, *discriminate validity*, *construct validity*, and *factor analysis*.

If you are new to the field of research and measurement, you may feel at this point that you would be hopelessly lost in trying to evaluate instruments in light of this evaluation question. However, even without formal training in measurement, you can check to see whether a researcher has addressed this issue. When researchers do this, they usually only briefly summarize the information, and these summaries are usually comprehensible to those who are new to the field. Examples 8.11.1 and 8.11.2 illustrate fairly typical summaries. Notice that they are exceptionally brief but contain references to publications where additional information may be obtained.

### Example 8.11.1[19]

*Statement regarding empirical validity of an instrument with a reference to its test manual[20] where more information may be obtained:*

The Test of Early Reading Ability-2 (TERS-2) (Reid, Hresko, & Hammill, 1989) is a norm-referenced assessment instrument.... The authors reported adequate construct validity including significant correlations (.61) with performance on the Basic Skills Inventory-Diagnostic Reading Subtest, high correlations with chronological age and school experience (.84), and successful differentiation of normal and learning-disabled students.

### Example 8.11.2[21]

*Statement regarding empirical validity of an instrument with a reference to where more information may be obtained:*

To assess binge drinking, we asked participants to respond either "yes" (= 1) or "no" (= 2) to the question "Have you had five or more drinks at any one time during the past three months?" This item has demonstrated very good validity in past studies (e.g., Taj, Devera-Sales, & Vinson, 1998).

Unfortunately, empirical validity is seldom addressed when researchers use newly developed instruments devised for their specific research studies. This is because an adequate empirical validity study is a major study in and of itself.

Note that it is traditional for researchers to address empirical validity only for instruments that yield scores, as opposed to instruments such as semistructured interviews.

---

[19] Sacks, C. H., & Mergendoller, J. R. (1997). The relationship between teachers' theoretical orientation toward reading and student outcomes in kindergarten children with different initial reading abilities. *American Educational Research Journal, 34,* 721–739.

[20] Note that the reference to Reid, Hresko, & Hammill, 1989, is a reference to the manual for the test.

[21] Wiscott, R., Kopera-Frye, K., & Begovic, A. (2002). Binge drinking in later life: Comparing young–old and old–old drinkers. *Psychology of Addictive Behaviors, 16,* 252–255.

### _____ 12. Do the researchers discuss obvious limitations of their instrumentation?

Very satisfactory  5  4  3  2  1  Very unsatisfactory  *or*  N/A  I/I

*Comment*: By discussing limitations of their instruments, researchers help consumers of research understand the extent to which the data presented in the results can be trusted. In Example 8.5.1 above, the researchers discuss how the limitations of using self-reports might have affected the outcomes of their study. In Example 8.12.1, the researchers also discuss the possibility that self-reports may not accurately reflect the levels of the variables they measured.

#### Example 8.12.1[22]

*Statement acknowledging a weakness in instrumentation*:

The exclusive use of individual self-report measures of sociocultural and relational variables, although common to this area of research, assessed participants' perceptions of pressures for thinness exerted on them by their environment and perceptions of social support offered to them by others, and not actual levels of these variables. Participants' perceptions of these variables may or may not be an accurate portrayal of reality.

If, in your judgment, there are no obvious limitations to the instrumentation described in a research report, a rating of N/A ("not applicable") should be made.

### _____ 13. Overall, is the instrumentation adequate?

Very satisfactory  5  4  3  2  1  Very unsatisfactory  *or*  N/A  I/I

*Comment*: The amount of information about instruments used in research that is reported in academic journals is often quite limited. The provision of references for obtaining additional information helps to overcome this problem.

Typically, if a researcher provides too little information for you to make an informed judgment and/or does not provide references where additional information can be obtained, you should give it a low rating on this evaluation question or respond that there is insufficient information (I/I). When considering instruments used in research, an I/I indicates an important flaw in the research.

---

[22] Tylka, T. L., & Subich, L. M. (2004). Examining a multidimensional model of eating disorder symptomatology among college women. *Journal of Counseling Psychology*, *51*, 314–328.

# Exercise for Chapter 8

## Part A

*Directions*: Answer the following questions.

1. Very briefly name three reasons why qualitative researchers tend to use multiple measures (such as interviews supplemented by observations).

2. Name two or three issues that some participants might regard as sensitive and, hence, difficult to measure. Answer this question with examples that are *not* mentioned in this book. (See the discussion of Evaluation Question 5.)

3. Have you ever changed your behavior because you knew (or thought) you were being observed? If yes, briefly describe how or why you were being observed and what behavior(s) you changed. (See Evaluation Question 6.)

4. According to this chapter, what is a reasonably high rate of agreement when two or more independent observers classify behavior?

5. For which of the following would it be more important to look at internal consistency using Cronbach's alpha? Explain your answer.

   A. For a single test of mathematics ability for first graders that yields a single score.
   B. For a single test of reading and mathematics abilities for first graders that yields a single score.

6. Suppose a researcher obtained a test-retest reliability coefficient of 0.86. According to this chapter, does this indicate adequate temporal stability? Explain.

7. Which type of validity is mentioned in this chapter as being an important issue in the evaluation of achievement tests?

## Part B

*Directions*: Locate three research reports of interest to you in academic journals. Evaluate the descriptions of the instruments in light of the evaluation questions in this chapter as well as any other considerations and concerns you may have. Select the one to which you gave the highest overall rating, and bring it to class for discussion. Be prepared to discuss both its strengths and weaknesses.

*Notes*:

# Chapter 9

# Evaluating Experimental Procedures

An experiment is a study in which treatments are given in order to determine their effects. For instance, one group of students might be trained how to use conflict-resolution techniques (the experimental group) while a control group is not given this training. Then, the students in both groups could be observed on the playground to determine whether the experimental group used more conflict-resolution techniques than the control group did.

The treatments (i.e., training versus no training) constitute what is known as the *independent variable*, which is sometimes called the stimulus or input variable. The resulting behavior on the playground constitutes the *dependent variable*, which is sometimes called the output or response variable.

Any study in which even a single treatment is given to just a single participant is an experiment as long as the purpose of the study is to determine the effects of the treatment on another variable. A study that does not meet this minimal condition is *not* an experiment. Thus, for example, a political poll in which questions are asked but no treatments are given is *not* an experiment and should *not* be referred to as such.

The following evaluation questions cover only the most important principles for the evaluation of experiments. To a large extent, the presentation is nontechnical. To become conversant with the technical terms and jargon associated with experimentation, consult any major research methods textbook.

___ **1. If two or more groups are compared, were individuals assigned at random to the groups?**

Very satisfactory  5  4  3  2  1  Very unsatisfactory  *or*  N/A  I/I

*Comment*: Assigning individuals at random to groups guarantees that there is no bias in the assignment. For instance, random assignment to two groups in the experiment on conflict-resolution training (mentioned at the beginning of this chapter) assures us that there is no bias, such as systematically assigning the less-aggressive children to the experimental group. Note that it is *not* safe to assume the assignment was done at random unless a researcher explicitly states that it was done, which is illustrated in

Example 9.1.1. Note that after the random assignment, repeated attempts were made to obtain the continuing participation of those assigned to the two experimental groups.

### Example 9.1.1

*Excerpt from three experiments with random assignment explicitly mentioned*:

Eighty clients enrolled in a managed care health plan who identified panic disorder as their primary presenting problem were randomly assigned to treatment by a therapist recently trained in a manual-based empirically supported psychotherapy…or a therapist conducting treatment as usual (TAU).[1]

The participants were randomly assigned to one of the three methylphenidate doses.[2]

Participants were randomly divided into 2 groups of 18….[3]

Note that assigning *individuals* to treatments at random is vastly superior to assigning previously existing *groups* to treatments at random. For instance, in educational research, it is not uncommon to assign one class to an experimental treatment and another class to serve as the control group. Because students are not ordinarily randomly assigned to classes, there may be systematic differences between the students in the two classes. For instance, one class might have more highly motivated students, another might have more parental involvement, and so on. Thus, you should *not* answer "yes" to this evaluation question unless *individuals* were assigned at random.

If you can answer "yes" to this evaluation question, the experiment you are evaluating is known as a *true experiment*. Note that this term does not imply that the experiment is perfect, as you will see when you apply other evaluation questions in this chapter. In other words, a *true experiment* has the very desirable characteristic of having individuals assigned to treatment and control conditions at random. The term does not refer to other criteria that should be applied when evaluating experiments.

### ___ 2. If two or more comparison groups were *not* formed at random, is there evidence that they were initially equal in important ways?

Very satisfactory   5   4   3   2   1   Very unsatisfactory   *or*   N/A   I/I

---

[1] Addis, M. E. et al. (2004). Effectiveness of cognitive-behavioral treatment for panic disorder versus treatment as usual in a managed care setting. *Journal of Consulting and Clinical Psychology, 72*, 625–635.
[2] Roehrs, T. et al. (2004). Reinforcing and subjective effects of methylphenidate dose and time in bed. *Experimental and Clinical Psychopharmacology, 12*, 180–189.
[3] Ward, G., & Tan, L. (2004). The effect of the length of to-be-reimbursed lists and intervening lists on free recall: A reexamination using overt rehearsal. *Journal of Experimental Psychology: Learning, Memory, and Cognition, 30*, 1196–1210.

*Comment*: Suppose a researcher wants to study the impact of a new third-grade reading program that is being used with all third graders in a school (the experimental group). To get a control group, the researcher will have to use third graders in another school.[4] Because students are not randomly assigned to schools, this experiment will get low marks on Evaluation Question 1. However, if the researcher selects a control school in which the first graders have standardized reading test scores similar to those in the experimental school and are similar in other important respects such as parents' socioeconomic status, some useful information may still be obtained.

Note, however, that having such evidence of similarity between groups is not as satisfactory as assigning individuals at random to groups. For instance, the children in the two schools in our example may be different in some important respect that the researcher has overlooked or has no information on. Perhaps the children's teachers in the experimental school are more experienced. Their experience in teaching, rather than the new reading program, might be the cause of any differences in reading achievement between the two groups.

When using two intact groups (such as two schools), it is important to give both a pretest and a posttest to measure the dependent variable. For instance, to evaluate the reading program, a researcher should give a pretest in reading, which will establish whether the two intact groups are initially similar on the dependent variable. Of course, the experiment will be more interpretable if they are initially similar.[5]

## ____ 3. If only a single participant or a single group is used, have the treatments been alternated?

Very satisfactory   5   4   3   2   1   Very unsatisfactory   *or*   N/A   I/I

*Comment*: Not all experiments involve the comparison of two or more groups that have been treated differently. Consider, for instance, a teacher who wants to try using increased praise for appropriate behaviors in the classroom to see if it reduces behaviors such as inappropriate out-of-seat behavior (IOSB). To conduct an experiment on this, the teacher could count the number of IOSBs for a week or two before administering the increased praise. This would yield what is called the *baseline data*. Suppose the teacher then introduces the extra praise and finds a decrease in the IOSBs. This might suggest that the extra praise *caused* the improvement. However, such a conclusion would be highly tenuous because children's environments are constantly changing in many ways and some other environmental influence (such as the school princi-

---

[4] As you may know, the use of two intact groups (groups that were already formed) with both a pretest and a posttest is known as a *quasi-experiment*—as opposed to a *true experiment*.

[5] If the groups are initially dissimilar, a researcher should consider locating another group that is more similar to serve as the control. If this is not possible, a statistical technique known as analysis of covariance can be used to adjust the posttest scores in light of the initial differences in pretest scores. Such a statistical adjustment can be risky if the assumptions underlying the test have been violated, a topic beyond the scope of this book.

pal scolding the students on the playground without the teacher's knowledge) might be the real cause of the change. A more definitive test would be for the teacher to reverse the treatment and go back to giving less praise, followed by another reversal to the higher-praise condition. If the data form the expected pattern, the teacher would have reasonable evidence that increased praise reduces IOSB.

Notice that in this experiment, the single group serves as a control group during the baseline, serves as the experimental group when the extra praise is initially given, serves as the control group again when the condition is reversed, and finally serves as the experimental group again when the extra praise is reintroduced. Such a design has this strength: The same children with the same backgrounds are both the experimental and control groups. (In a two-group experiment, the children in one group may be different from the children in the other group in some important way that affects the outcome of the experiment.) The major drawback of a single-group design is that the same children are being exposed to multiple treatments, which may lead to unnatural reactions. How does a child feel when some weeks he or she gets extra praise for appropriate behaviors but other weeks does not? Obviously, such reactions could confound the results of the experiment.

If two classes were available for the type of experiment being considered, a teacher could use what is called a *multiple baseline design*, in which the initial extra-praise condition is started on a different week for each group. If the pattern of decreased IOSB under the extra praise condition holds up across both groups, the causal conclusion would be even stronger than when only one group was used at one point in time.

The type of experimentation being discussed under this evaluation question is often referred to as *single-subject research* or *behavior analysis*. When a researcher has only a single participant or one intact group that cannot be divided at random into two or more groups, such a design can provide useful information about causality.

## ____ 4. Are the treatments described in sufficient detail?

Very satisfactory   5   4   3   2   1   Very unsatisfactory   *or*   N/A   I/I

*Comment*: Researchers should give rather thorough descriptions of the treatments that were administered because the sole purpose of an experiment is to estimate the effects of the treatments on dependent variables. The reader should be able to picture what was done and by whom. If the treatments are complex, such as two types of therapy in clinical psychology applied for an extended period of time, researchers should provide references to additional publications where detailed accounts can be found, if possible. In Example 9.4.1, the researchers begin by giving references for the experimental task and then describe how it was used in their study. Only a portion of their detailed description of the treatment is shown in the example.

**Example 9.4.1[6]**

*Excerpt showing references for more information on experimental treatment followed by a detailed description (partial description shown here):*

The negotiation task was one previously used by Van Kleef et al. (2004) and adapted from De Dreu and Van Lange (1995; see also Hilty & Carnevale, 1993). The task captures the main characteristics of real-life negotiation (i.e., multiple issues differing in utility to the negotiator, information about one's own payoffs only, and the typical offer-counteroffer sequence). In the current version, participants learned that they would be assigned the role of either buyer or seller of a consignment of mobile phones (all participants were assigned to the seller role) and that their objective was to negotiate the price, the warranty period, and the duration of the free-service contract of the phones. Participants were then presented with a payoff chart....

---

## ___ 5. If the treatments were administered by individuals other than the researcher, were they properly trained?

Very satisfactory   5   4   3   2   1   Very unsatisfactory   *or*   N/A   I/I

*Comment*: Researchers often rely on other individuals, such as graduate assistants, teachers, and psychologists, to administer the treatments they are using in an experiment. When this is the case, it is desirable for the researcher to assure the readers that they were properly trained. Otherwise, it is possible that the treatments were modified in some unknown way. Example 9.5.1 shows a statement regarding the training of student therapists who administered treatments in an experiment. Note that such statements are typically brief.

**Example 9.5.1[7]**

*Excerpt on training those who administered the treatments:*

Student therapists received 54 hr of training in EFT–AS [emotion-focused therapy for adult survivors of child abuse]. This consisted of reviewing the treatment manual and videotapes of therapy sessions with expert therapists, as well as supervised peer skills practice and three sessions of therapy with volunteer "practice" clients.

---

[6] Van Kleef, G. A., De Dreu, C. K. W., & Manstead, A. S. R. (2004). The interpersonal effects of emotions in negotiations: A motivated information processing approach. *Journal of Personality and Social Psychology, 87*, 510–528.

[7] Paivio, S. C., Holowaty, K. A. M., & Hall, I. E. (2004). The influence of therapist adherence and competence on client reprocessing of child abuse memories. *Psychotherapy: Theory, Research, Practice, Training, 41*, 56–68.

**____ 6. If the treatments were administered by individuals other than the researcher, was there a check to see if they administered the treatments properly?**

Very satisfactory  5  4  3  2  1  Very unsatisfactory  *or*  N/A  I/I

*Comment*: Even if those who administered the treatments were trained, they normally should be monitored. This is especially true for long and complex treatment cycles. For instance, if psychologists will be trying out new techniques with clients over a period of several months, it would be desirable to spot-check their efforts to determine whether they are applying their training properly. This can be done by directly observing them or by questioning them.

**____ 7. If each treatment group had a different person administering a treatment, has the researcher tried to eliminate the "personal effect"?**

Very satisfactory  5  4  3  2  1  Very unsatisfactory  *or*  N/A  I/I

*Comment*: Suppose that the purpose of an experiment is to compare the effectiveness of three methods for teaching decoding skills in first-grade reading instruction. If each method is used by a different teacher, differences in the teachers (such as ability to build rapport with students, level of enthusiasm, ability to build effective relationships with parents) may cause any observed differences in achievement (i.e., they may have had a "personal effect" on the outcome). One solution to this problem is to have each of the three methods used by a large number of teachers, with the teachers assigned at random to the methods. If such a large-scale study is not possible, another solution is to have each teacher use all three methods. In other words, Teacher A could use Methods X, Y, and Z at different points in time with different children; the other two teachers would do likewise. When the results are averaged, the "personal effect" of each teacher will have contributed to the average scores earned under each of the three methods.

**____ 8. Except for differences in the treatments, were all other conditions the same in the experimental and control groups?**

Very satisfactory  5  4  3  2  1  Very unsatisfactory  *or*  N/A  I/I

*Comment*: The results of an experiment can be influenced by many variables other than the independent variable. For instance, if experimental and control groups are treated at different times of the day or in different rooms in a building (where one room is noisy and the other is not), these factors might influence the outcome of an experiment. We say that variables such as these are *confounding variables* because they confound the interpretation.

Many researchers are silent on whether all other conditions were controlled by making them the same for all groups in an experiment. Undoubtedly, many of them believe that readers will assume that the researcher is aware of this requirement for a good experiment and has met it without having to discuss it. In other cases, you may have some legitimate concerns about this issue. For example, if a researcher tells you that the experimental treatment was administered to children in one teacher's class while the children in another teacher's class served as controls, you may have concerns about the comparability of the two teachers' classrooms.

### ____ 9. When appropriate, have the researchers considered possible "demand characteristics"?

Very satisfactory  5  4  3  2  1  Very unsatisfactory  *or*  N/A  I/I

*Comment*: If participants know the true, exact purpose of an experiment, their responses may be influenced by this knowledge. For example, in a study on the effects of a film showing negative consequences of drinking alcohol, the experimental group participants might report more negative attitudes toward alcohol simply because they know the researcher has hypothesized that this will happen. In other words, sometimes participants try to give researchers what they think the researchers expect. This is known as a demand characteristic. It is called this because it operates as though a researcher is subtly demanding a certain outcome.

Certain types of instruments are more prone to the effects of demand characteristics than others. Self-report measures (such as self-reported attitudes toward alcohol) are especially sensitive to them. When interpreting the results obtained with such instruments, researchers should consider whether any differences are due to the "demands" of the experiments. One way to overcome this difficulty is to supplement self-report measures with other measures such as reports by friends or significant others.

On the other hand, an achievement test is less sensitive to the "demands" of an experiment because students who do not have the skills being tested will not be successful on a test even if he or she wants to please the researcher by producing the desired behavior. Likewise, many physical measures are insensitive to this type of influence. In an experiment on methods for reducing cocaine use, for instance, a participant will not be able to alter the results of a blood test for the presence of cocaine.

### ____ 10. Is the setting for the experiment "natural"?

Very satisfactory  5  4  3  2  1  Very unsatisfactory  *or*  N/A  I/I

*Comment*: Sometimes, researchers conduct experiments in unnatural settings. When they do this, they limit their study's *external validity*, that is, what is found in the unnatural environment of a study may not be found in more natural settings (i.e., the finding may not be valid in a more natural setting).

Experiments conducted in laboratory settings often have poor external validity. Notice the unnatural aspects of Example 9.10.1. First, the amount and type of alcoholic beverages were assigned (rather than being selected by the participants as they would in a natural setting). Second, the female was a cohort of the experimenter (not someone the males were actually dating). Third, the setting was a laboratory, where the males would be likely to suspect that their behavior was being monitored in some way. While the researchers have achieved a high degree of physical control over the experimental setting, they have sacrificed external validity in the process.

### Example 9.10.1
*Experiment with poor external validity*:

A research team was interested in the effects of alcohol consumption on aggressiveness in males when dating. In their experiment, some of the males were given moderate amounts of beer to consume. Then all males were observed interacting with a female cohort of the experimenters. The interactions took place in a laboratory on a college campus, and observations were made through a one-way mirror.

___ **11. Has the researcher distinguished between *random selection* and *random assignment*?**

Very satisfactory   5   4   3   2   1   Very unsatisfactory   *or*   N/A   I/I

*Comment*: The desirability of using *random selection* to obtain samples from which we can generalize with confidence to larger populations was discussed in Chapter 6. Such selection is highly desirable in any study—whether it is an experiment or not. *Random assignment*, on the other hand, refers to the process of assigning participants to the various treatment conditions (i.e., to the treatments, including any control condition).

Note that in any given experiment, *selection* may or may not be random. Likewise, *assignment* may or may not be random. Figure 9.11.1 illustrates the ideal situation where first there is random selection from a population of interest to obtain a sample. This is followed by random assignment of individuals to treatment conditions.

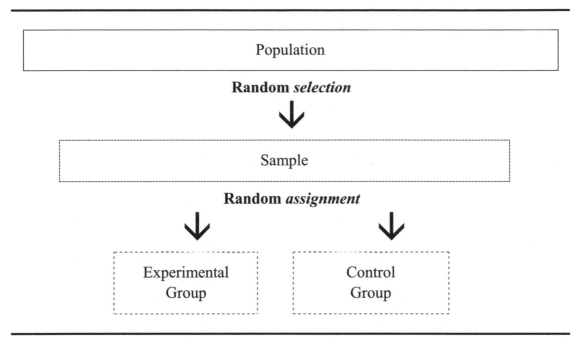

*Figure 9.11.1.*   Ideal combination of random selection and random assignment.

When discussing the generalizability of the results of an experiment, a researcher should do so in light of the type of *selection* used. In other words, a properly selected sample (ideally, selected at random) allows for more confidence when generalizing the results to a population. On the other hand, when discussing the comparability of the two groups, a researcher should consider the type of *assignment* used. In other words, proper assignment to a group (ideally, assigned at random) increases our confidence that the two groups were initially equal—permitting a valid comparison of the outcomes of treatments and control conditions.

### ___ 12. Has the researcher used ethical and politically acceptable treatments?

Very satisfactory   5   4   3   2   1   Very unsatisfactory   *or*   N/A   I/I

*Comment*: This evaluation question is applicable primarily to experiments in applied areas such as education, clinical psychology, social work, and medicine. For example, has the researcher used treatments to promote classroom discipline that will be acceptable to parents, teachers, and the community? Or, has the researcher used methods such as moderate corporal punishment by teachers, which will probably be unacceptable to many people?

A low mark on this question means that the experiment is unlikely to have an impact in the applied area in which it was conducted.

**____ 13. Overall, was the experiment properly conducted?**

Very satisfactory  5  4  3  2  1  Very unsatisfactory  *or*  N/A  I/I

*Comment*: Rate the overall quality of the experimental procedures based on the answers to the evaluation questions in this chapter and any other concerns you may have.

# Concluding Comment

This chapter presents a commonsense approach to the evaluation of experiments. For those of you who are using this book in coordination with a traditional research methods textbook, a few comments on terminology are in order. First, most textbooks distinguish between *internal validity* and *external validity*. We say that an experiment has high *internal validity* when the differences in treatment are the only logical possible cause for any observed differences among groups. Evaluation Questions 1 through 8 in this chapter deal with this issue. On the other hand, we say that an experiment has high *external validity* when we have confidence that the results apply to the population to which the researcher wishes to generalize. Evaluation Questions 9 through 11 deal with this second issue. Evaluation Question 11 deals with both these issues because *random selection* contributes to a study's external validity while *random assignment* contributes to its internal validity.

As a final matter, an experiment to which participants are assigned at random is said to be a *true experiment*. An experiment in which groups are formed in a nonrandom fashion but on which we have data suggesting that they are initially equal is said to be a *quasi-experiment*.[8] Experiments of lesser quality (such as not having a control condition or comparing two groups that are not formed at random *and* for which there are no data on the initial equality of the groups) are said to be *pre-experiments*.

# Exercise for Chapter 9

**Part A**

*Directions*: Answer the following questions.

1. In an experiment, the treatments constitute what is known as
   A. an independent variable.   B. a dependent variable.

---

[8] Quasi-experimental designs include single-subject/behavior analysis designs that have reversals (see Evaluation Question 3). These are not true experiments by definition because they do not include random assignment of individuals to groups.

2. Which of the following is described in this chapter as being vastly superior to the other?
   A. Assigning previously existing *groups* to treatments at random.
   B. Assigning *individuals* to treatments at random.

3. Suppose a psychology professor conducted an experiment in which one of her sections of Introduction to Social Psychology was assigned to be the experimental group and the other section served as the control group during a given semester. The experimental group used computer-assisted instruction while the control group received instruction via a traditional lecture/discussion method. Although both groups are taking a course in social psychology during the same semester, the two groups might be initially different in other ways. Speculate on what some of the differences might be. (See Evaluation Question 2.)

4. In this chapter, what is described as a strength of an experimental design in which one group serves as both the treatment group and its own control group?

5. Very briefly describe how the "personal effect" might confound an experiment.

6. In your opinion, is it ethical to disguise the purpose of an experiment from participants? Explain.

7. Explain what it means to say that a particular experiment lacks *external validity*.

8. Briefly explain how *random selection* differs from *random assignment*.

9. Is it possible to have *nonrandom selection* yet still have *random assignment* in an experiment? Explain.

## Part B

*Directions*: Locate several experiments on topics of interest to you in academic journals. Evaluate them in light of the evaluation questions in this chapter as well as any other considerations and concerns you may have. Select the one to which you gave the highest overall rating and bring it to class for discussion. Be prepared to discuss both its strengths and weaknesses.

*Notes*:

# Chapter 10

# Evaluating Analysis and Results Sections: Quantitative Research

This chapter discusses the evaluation of analysis and Results sections in *quantitative research* reports. These almost always contain statistics that summarize the data that were collected, such as means, standard deviations, and correlation coefficients. These types of statistics are known as *descriptive statistics*. The Results sections of quantitative research reports also usually contain *inferential statistics*, which help in making inferences from the sample that was actually studied to the population from which the sample was drawn.

In this chapter, it is assumed that you have basic knowledge of elementary statistical methods.

Note that the evaluation of analysis and Results sections of *qualitative research* reports is covered in the next chapter.

## ___ 1. Have appropriate descriptive statistics been reported?

Very satisfactory  5  4  3  2  1  Very unsatisfactory  *or*  N/A  I/I

*Comment*: By far, the most widely reported descriptive statistics are percentages, means, and standard deviations.

When reporting percentages, it is important for researchers to also report the underlying number of cases for each percentage. Otherwise, the results can be misleading. Consider Example 10.1.1, which contains only percentages. The percentage decrease in this example seems dramatic. However, when the underlying numbers of cases (whose symbol is *n*) are shown, as in Example 10.1.2, it becomes clear that the percentage represents only a very small decrease in absolute terms (i.e., a decrease from 4 students to 2 students).

### Example 10.1.1
*Percentage reported without underlying number of cases (potentially misleading)*:

Since the end of the Cold War, interest in Russian language studies has decreased dramatically. For instance, at Zaneville Language Institute, the number of students majoring in Russian has decreased by 50% from a decade earlier.

### Example 10.1.2

*Percentage reported with underlying number of cases (not misleading)*:

Since the end of the Cold War, interest in Russian language studies has decreased dramatically. For instance, at Zaneville Language Institute, the number of students majoring in Russian has decreased by 50% from a decade earlier ($n = 4$ in 1995, $n = 2$ in 2005).

The *mean*, which is the most commonly reported average, should be used only when a distribution is *not* highly skewed. In other words, it should be used only when a distribution is approximately symmetrical. A skewed distribution is one in which there are some extreme scores on one side of the distribution (such as some very high scores without some very low scores to counterbalance them). Example 10.1.3 shows a skewed distribution. It is skewed because there is a very high score of 310 which is not balanced out by a very low score at the lower end of the distribution of scores. This is known as a distribution that is *skewed to the right.*[1] The mean, which is supposed to represent the central tendency of the entire group of scores, has been pulled up by a single very high score, resulting in a mean of 82.45, which is higher than all of the scores except the highest one (the score of 310).

### Example 10.1.3

*A skewed distribution (skewed to the right) and a misleading mean*:

Scores: 55, 55, 56, 57, 58, 60, 61, 63, 66, 66, 310
Mean = 82.45, standard deviation = 75.57

The raw scores for which a mean was calculated are very seldom included in research reports. However, a couple of simple computations using only the mean and standard deviation (which are usually reported) can reveal whether the mean was misapplied to a distribution that is highly skewed to the right. These are the calculations:

1. Round the mean and standard deviation to whole numbers (to keep the computations simple). Thus, the rounded mean is 82, and the rounded standard deviation is 76.
2. Multiply the standard deviation by 2 (i.e., $76 \times 2 = 152$).
3. *SUBTRACT* the result of Step 2 from the mean (i.e., $82 - 152 = -70$).

If the result of Step 3 is lower than the lowest possible score, which is usually zero, the distribution is highly skewed to the right.[2] (In this example, −70 is much

---

[1] A distribution that is skewed to the right is also sometimes said to have a "positive skew."

[2] You may recall from a statistics course that in a normal, symmetrical distribution, there are three standard deviation units on each side of the mean. Thus, there should be 3 standard deviation units on both sides of the mean in a distribution that is not skewed. In this example, we have seen that there are not even 2 standard deviation units to the left of the mean (because we multiplied the standard deviation by 2). Even if you do not understand this theory, you can still apply the simple steps described here to identify the misapplication of the mean. Note that there are precise statistical methods for detecting a skew. However, to use them, you need to have the original scores, which are almost never available to consumers of research.

lower than zero). This indicates that the mean was applied to a distribution that is skewed to the right, resulting in a misleading value for an average (i.e., an average that is misleadingly high).[3] This type of inappropriate selection of an average is rather common, perhaps because researchers often compute the mean and standard deviation for a set of scores without first considering whether the distribution of scores is skewed.

It is also easy to detect the misapplication of the mean to describe a distribution that is highly *skewed to the left*.[4] Example 10.1.4 illustrates this, with a very low score of 3 without a very high score on the right to balance it out. This distribution has a mean score of 54.54, which is lower than all the other scores in the distribution except for the extremely low score of 3. Thus, 54.54 does not appropriately represent the central tendency of the distribution.

### Example 10.1.4

*A skewed distribution (skewed to the left) and a misleading mean*:

Scores: 3, 55, 55, 56, 57, 58, 60, 61, 63, 66, 66
Mean = 54.54, standard deviation = 17.56

When the raw scores are not available, you can determine if the distribution is skewed to the left by using the mean and standard deviation in the following, which are illustrated for Example 10.1.4:

1.  Round the mean and standard deviations to whole numbers (to keep the computations simple). Thus, the rounded mean is 54, and the rounded standard deviation is 18.
2.  Multiply the standard deviation by 2 (i.e., $18 \times 2 = 36$).
3.  *ADD* the result of Step 2 to the mean (i.e., $54 + 36 = 90$).

If the result of Step 3 is higher than the highest score, the distribution is highly skewed to the left. (In this example, the result of Step 3 is 90, which is higher than the highest score of 66.) This indicates that the mean was applied to a distribution highly skewed to the left, resulting in a misleading low value for an average.

If you detect that a mean has been computed for a highly skewed distribution by performing the two sets of calculations described above, there is nothing you can do to correct it short of contacting the researcher to request the raw scores.[5] If this is not feasible, you need to interpret the mean with great caution, and give the report a low mark on this evaluation question.

---

[3] This procedure will not detect all highly skewed distributions. If the result of Step 3 is lower than the lowest score obtained by any participant, the distribution is also skewed. However, researchers seldom report the lowest score obtained by participants.

[4] A distribution that is skewed to the left is also sometimes said to have a "negative skew."

[5] With the raw scores, you could then compute the *median*, which is the appropriate average to use with skewed distributions. To obtain the median for a set of scores, put them in order from low to high and count to the middle score, which is the median. In Example 10.1.4, there are 11 scores, and the middle score is 58, which is the median. Notice that this is in the center of the set of scores.

## ___ 2. If any differences are statistically significant and small, have the researchers noted that they are small?

Very satisfactory   5   4   3   2   1   Very unsatisfactory   *or*   N/A   I/I

*Comment*: Statistically significant differences are sometimes very small. (See Appendix C for an explanation of this point.) When this is the case, it is a good idea for a researcher to point this out. Obviously, a very small but statistically significant difference will be interpreted differently from a large and statistically significant difference. Example 10.2.1 illustrates how this might be pointed out.[6]

### Example 10.2.1
*Description of a small but statistically significant difference*:

Although the difference between the means of the experimental group ($M$ = 24.55) and control group ($M$ = 23.65) was statistically significant ($t$ = 2.075, $p$ < .05), the small size of the difference, in absolute terms, suggests that the effects of the experimental treatment were weak.

This evaluation question is posed because researchers sometimes incorrectly believe that simply because a difference is statistically significant, it must be large and important. When they do this, they fail to understand that a significant difference is merely one that is unlikely to have been produced by chance. Note that there are no mathematical formulas (or tests) to determine the practical importance of a difference.

## ___ 3. Is the Results section a cohesive essay?

Very satisfactory   5   4   3   2   1   Very unsatisfactory   *or*   N/A   I/I

*Comment*: The Results section should be an essay—not just a collection of statistics. In other words, researchers should describe results in paragraphs, each of which describes some aspect of the results. These paragraphs generally will contain statistics. The essay usually should be organized around the research hypotheses, research questions, or research purposes. See the example under the next guideline.

## ___ 4. Does the researcher refer back to the research hypotheses, purposes, or questions originally stated in the Introduction?

Very satisfactory   5   4   3   2   1   Very unsatisfactory   *or*   N/A   I/I

---

[6] An increasingly popular statistic, *effect size*, is designed to draw readers' attention to the size of any significant difference. In general terms, it indicates by how many standard deviations two groups differ from each other. Unfortunately, its use is not very widespread to date.

*Comment*: This guideline may not be applicable to a very short research report with a single hypothesis, question, or purpose. When there are several of these, however, readers should be shown how different elements of the results relate to the specific hypotheses, questions, or purposes, as illustrated in Example 10.4.1. The authors of this example had three hypotheses and refer to them by their ordinal position ("1," "2," and "3"). They also indicate the content of each hypothesis (e.g., Hypothesis 3: The women shown in the photos were viewed as less feminine when described as entrepreneurs than as managers). The tables referred to in the example are not shown here.

### Example 10.4.1[7]
*Results discussed in terms of specific hypotheses*:

Results offered support for Hypothesis 1. As predicted, women shown in standard-format photos received higher ratings on personal traits when they were described as being entrepreneurs than when they were described as being managers. In more specific terms, the women were rated significantly higher on two traits—decisiveness and career seriousness—when described as entrepreneurs (Hypothesis 1).  See Table 1 for mean ratings.

The same pattern was obtained through the perceived causes of their success (i.e., attributions–Hypothesis 2)…. Their success was attributed less to luck and more to specific skills (i.e., social skills–Hypothesis 2). See Table 2.

Finally, as predicted by Hypothesis 3, the women shown in the photos were viewed as less feminine when described as entrepreneurs than as managers. See Table 3.

### ___ 5. When there are a number of related statistics, have they been presented in a table?

Very satisfactory  5  4  3  2  1  Very unsatisfactory  *or*  N/A  I/I

*Comment*: Even when there are as few as six related statistics, a table can be helpful. For instance, consider Example 10.5.1, in which percentages and numbers of cases (*n*) are presented in a paragraph. Compare it with Example 10.5.2, in which the same ten percentages are reported in tabular form. Clearly, the tabular form is easier to follow.

---

[7] Modified from Baron, R. A., Markman, G. D., & Hirsa, A. (2001). Perceptions of women and men as entrepreneurs: Evidence for differential effects of attributional augmenting. *Journal of Applied Psychology, 86*, 923–929.

### Example 10.5.1[8]

*Too many statistics presented in a paragraph (compare with Example 10.5.2, which presents the same statistics in a table):*

Two percent of the girls ($n = 8$) and 2% of the boys ($n = 8$) reported that they were "Far too skinny." Boys and girls were also identical in response to the choice "A little skinny" (8%, $n = 41$ for girls and 8%, $n = 34$ for boys). For "Just right," a larger percentage of boys (76%, $n = 337$) than girls (70%, $n = 358$) responded. For "A little fat," the responses were 18% ($n = 92$) and 13% ($n = 60$) for girls and boys, respectively. Also, a slightly higher percentage of girls than boys reported being "Far too fat" with 2% ($n = 12$) for girls and 1% ($n = 6$) for boys.

### Example 10.5.2

Table 1
*Answers to question on self-perceived weight*

| Answer | Girls | | Boys | |
|---|---|---|---|---|
| | % | n | % | n |
| Far too skinny | 2 | 8 | 2 | 8 |
| A little skinny | 8 | 41 | 8 | 34 |
| Just right | 70 | 358 | 76 | 337 |
| A little fat | 18 | 92 | 13 | 60 |
| Far too fat | 2 | 12 | 1 | 6 |

## ___ 6. If there are tables, are their highlights discussed in the narrative of the Results section?

Very satisfactory  5  4  3  2  1  Very unsatisfactory  *or*  N/A  I/I

*Comment*: Researchers should point out the important highlights of their statistical tables, as illustrated in Example 10.6.1, which shows part of the discussion of the statistics in Example 10.5.2 above. Note that only *highlights* of the statistics should be presented. To repeat them all in paragraph form would be redundant.

When there are large tables, pointing out the highlights can be especially helpful for consumers of the research.

### Example 10.6.1[9]

*Highlights of Example 10.5.2 pointed out*:

The same percentage of boys as girls (10%) perceived themselves as a little or far too skinny, while 20% of the girls and 14% of the boys perceived themselves

---

[8] Adapted from Erling, A., & Hwang, C. P. (2004). Body-esteem in Swedish 10-year-old children. *Perceptual and Motor Skills*, *99*, 437–444. In the research report, the statistics are reported in tabular form, as recommended here.
[9] Ibid.

as a little or far too fat (see Table 1). Of the 104 girls who perceived themselves as fat (a little fat or far too fat), only....

### ___ 7. Have the researchers presented descriptive statistics before presenting the results of inferential tests?

Very satisfactory  5  4  3  2  1  Very unsatisfactory  *or*  N/A  I/I

*Comment*: Descriptive statistics include frequencies, percentages, averages (usually the mean or median), and measures of variability (usually the standard deviation or interquartile range). In addition, correlation coefficients (usually the Pearson $r$) describe the direction and strength of relationships.

Inferential statistics determine the probability that any differences among descriptive statistics are due to chance (random sampling error). Obviously, it makes no sense to discuss the results of a test on descriptive statistics unless the descriptive statistics have first been presented. Failure on this evaluation question is very rare.

### ___ 8. Overall, is the presentation of the results comprehensible?

Very satisfactory  5  4  3  2  1  Very unsatisfactory  *or*  N/A  I/I

*Comment*: Even when the analysis is complex and advanced statistical methods have been applied, the essay that describes the results should be comprehensible to any intelligent layperson. Specifically, the essay should describe the results conceptually using everyday language while presenting for consumers of research who wish to consider the statistical results.

### ___ 9. Overall, is the presentation of the results adequate?

Very satisfactory  5  4  3  2  1  Very unsatisfactory  *or*  N/A  I/I

*Comment*: Rate this evaluation question after considering your answers to the earlier ones in this chapter and any additional considerations and concerns you may have.

# Exercise for Chapter 10

**Part A**

*Directions*: Answer the following questions.

1. When reporting percentages, what else is it important for researchers to present?

2. Should the mean be used to report the average of a highly skewed distribution?

3. Suppose you read that the mean equals 10.0 and the standard deviation equals 6.0. Is the distribution skewed? Explain.

4. Are statistically significant differences sometimes small differences?

5. Should the Results section be an essay *or* should it be only a collection of statistics?

6. According to this chapter, is it ever desirable to restate hypotheses that were originally stated in the Introduction of a research report? Explain.

7. If statistical results are presented in a table, should all the entries in the table be discussed? Explain.

8. Should descriptive statistics *or* inferential tests be reported first in Results sections?


**Part B**

*Directions*: Locate several quantitative research reports of interest to you in academic journals. Read them and evaluate the descriptions of the results in light of the evaluation questions in this chapter as well as any other considerations and concerns you may have. Select the one to which you gave the highest overall rating and bring it to class for discussion. Be prepared to discuss both its strengths and weaknesses.

# Chapter 11

# Evaluating Analysis and Results Sections: Qualitative Research

Because human judgment is central in the analysis of qualitative data, there is much more subjectivity in the analysis of qualitative data than in the analysis of quantitative data. Because the methods of analysis are quite different for the two types of research, they are dealt with in separate chapters (see Chapter 10 for evaluation questions for quantitative analysis and Results sections of research reports). Consult Appendix A for additional information on the differences between qualitative and quantitative research.

## ___ 1. Were the data analyzed independently by two or more individuals?

Very satisfactory  5  4  3  2  1  Very unsatisfactory  *or*  N/A  I/I

*Comment*: As a general rule, the results of qualitative research are considered more trustworthy when the responses of participants are independently analyzed by two or more individuals. Specifically, this means that the individuals initially code and/or categorize the responses without consulting with each other. Then, they compare the results of their analyses and discuss any discrepancies in an effort to reach a consensus. Doing this assures consumers of research that the results represent more than just the impressions of one individual, which might be idiosyncratic. Examples 11.1.1, 11.1.2, and 11.1.3 illustrate how this process might be described in a research report.

### Example 11.1.1[1]
*Independent analysis by two researchers*:

Two independent research psychologists developed a list of *domains* or *topic areas* based on the content of the discussions and the focus group questions used to organize information into similar topics. Once each reviewer had independently identified their domains, the two reviewers compared their separate lists of domains until consensus was reached.

---

[1] Williams, J. K., Wyatt, G. E., Resell, J., Peterson, J., & Asuan-O'Brien, A. (2004). Psychosocial issues among gay- and non-gay-identifying HIV-seropositive African American and Latino MSM. *Cultural Diversity and Ethnic Minority Psychology, 10*, 268–286.

### Example 11.1.2[2]

*Independent analysis by three researchers [italics added for emphasis]:*

The interview notes were analyzed by three raters: myself and two doctoral students.... Each quote from the notes was assigned a descriptive category according to its content. The notes were organized into groups with the same category labels. Some similar groups were combined under inclusive categories. The main categories that were derived from the interviews, the coping strategies, mechanisms, and resources were then defined. In the next stage, the information from the interviews was coded according to the defined categories, evaluated, and summarized to describe the realities as accurately as possible. *Each of the three raters independently analyzed the type of coping strategies and categories. Any disagreement between raters was discussed and resolved.* The interrater reliability was high.

### Example 11.1.3[3]

*Independent analysis by two researchers:*

Themes were coded independently by the two coders and were discussed, and differences were clarified until consensus was reached.

___ **2. Did the researchers seek feedback from experienced individuals and auditors before finalizing the results?**

Very satisfactory  5  4  3  2  1  Very unsatisfactory  *or*  N/A  I/I

*Comment:* Seeking feedback helps to ensure the trustworthiness of the results. Example 11.2.1 is drawn from a report of research on incarcerated young men. The researchers had their preliminary results reviewed by two other individuals who had experienced incarceration (independent experienced individuals).

### Example 11.2.1[4]

*Feedback from independent experienced individuals:*

Finally, the data summary was reviewed by two individuals with a personal history of incarceration who were not involved in the data analytic process for critique of the face validity of the findings. Their feedback was incorporated into the discussion of our findings.

---

[2] Westman, M. (2004). Strategies for coping with business trips: A qualitative exploratory study. *International Journal of Stress Management, 11,* 167–176.

[3] Dillon, C. O., Liem, J. H., & Gore, S. (2003). Navigating disrupted transitions: Getting back on track after dropping out of high school. *American Journal of Orthopsychiatry, 73,* 429–440.

[4] Seal, D. W. et al. (2004). A qualitative study of substance use and sexual behavior among 18- to 29-year-old men while incarcerated in the United States. *Health Education & Behavior, 31,* 775–789.

Often, researchers seek feedback on their preliminary results from content-area experts who were not involved in conducting the research. The technical name for such a person in qualitative research is an *auditor*. Example 11.2.2 describes the work of an auditor in a research project.

### Example 11.2.2[5]

*Feedback from a content-area expert (i.e., auditor):*

At three separate points…, the work of the analysis team was reviewed by an auditor. The first point came after domains had been agreed upon, the second point came after core ideas had been identified, and the third point came after the cross-analysis. In each case, the auditor made suggestions to the team regarding the names and ideas the team was working on. Adjustments were made after the team reached consensus on the feedback given by the auditor. Examples of feedback given by the auditor included suggestions on the wording of domain and category names and a request for an increased amount of specificity in the core ideas put forth by the team members. The auditor was a Caucasian female faculty member in the social psychology discipline whose research is focused in the area of domestic violence.

The use of outside experts helps to assure consumers of research that the results of the analysis are not unduly subjective, which is mentioned in the first sentence of Example 11.2.3. In this example, the outside experts (i.e., auditors) are referred to as "consultants."

### Example 11.2.3[6]

*Feedback from outside experts (i.e., consultants):*

I used two consultants to monitor the influence of my subjectivity on the data. The first consultant shadowed and challenged the research process by independently listening to the audiotaped interviews, writing reflections on the interviews, substantiating the determination of the essential themes, and reviewing the findings against the associated quotes from the transcripts. The second consultant was a specialist in hermeneutic phenomenology. She reviewed methodological procedures, the essential themes, and descriptions of the themes.

---

[5] Wettersten, K. B. et al. (2004). Freedom through self-sufficiency: A qualitative examination of the impact of domestic violence on the working lives of women in shelter. *Journal of Counseling Psychology, 51,* 447–462.

[6] Armour, M. P. (2002). Journey of family members of homicide victims: A qualitative study of their post-homicide experience. *American Journal of Orthopsychiatry, 72,* 372–382.

## ___ 3. Did the researchers seek feedback from the participants (i.e., use member checking) before finalizing the results?

Very satisfactory   5   4   3   2   1   Very unsatisfactory   *or*   N/A   I/I

*Comment*: As you know from Evaluation Question 2, seeking feedback helps to ensure the trustworthiness of the results. When researchers seek feedback on their preliminary results from the participants in the research, the process is called *member checking*. Using member checking is not always feasible, especially with very young participants and participants with limited cognitive abilities. The authors of Example 11.3.1 used member checks.

### Example 11.3.1[7]

*Feedback from "members" (i.e., member checking by participants)*:

In the final phase of data analysis, participants were sent a draft of the manuscript being prepared for publication to solicit feedback regarding accuracy, usefulness of the model in describing their experience, and protection of their identities. This process, termed *member checking*, is used to verify credibility of data analysis (a form of trustworthiness; Lincoln & Guba, 1985). Comments from the four participants who responded were incorporated into the final manuscript as appropriate.

## ___ 4. Did the researchers name the method of analysis they used and provide (a) reference(s) for it?

Very satisfactory   5   4   3   2   1   Very unsatisfactory   *or*   N/A   I/I

*Comment*: Various methods for analyzing qualitative data have been suggested. Researchers should name the particular method they followed. Often, they name it and provide one or more references where additional information can be obtained. Examples 11.4.1 and 11.4.2 illustrate this for two widely used methods.

### Example 11.4.1[8]

*Naming "grounded theory" as the method of analysis with references for more information on the method [italics added for emphasis]*:

Grounded theory is a methodology for developing theory that is grounded in data gathered in diverse ways, but systematically collected and analyzed. Theory is mostly generated through coding techniques (i.e., open coding, axial coding,

---

[7] Gomez, M. J. et al. (2001). Voces Abriendo Caminos (Voices Forging Paths): A qualitative study of the career development of notable Latinas. *Journal of Counseling Psychology*, *48*, 286–300.

[8] Borrayo, E. A., & Jenkins, S. R. (2003). Feeling frugal: Socioeconomic status, acculturation, and cultural health beliefs among women of Mexican descent. *Cultural Diversity and Ethnic Minority Psychology*, *9*, 197–206.

and selective coding) that encourage the constant comparison of the data with an emerging conceptual framework of plausible relationships between theoretical concepts. The data collection and analytic procedures occur in stages that are not discrete and may not follow each other in a strict linear sequence. As noted by Strauss (1987), the procedures for discovering, verifying, and formulating theory are used both sequentially and simultaneously throughout the research process. *For a more detailed explanation of grounded theory data analysis, refer to Glaser and Strauss (1967) and Strauss and Corbin (1990).*

### Example 11.4.2[9]

*Naming "consensual qualitative research" as the method of analysis with references for more information on the method*:

Analyses consisted of using consensual qualitative research (CQR) methodology (Bogdan & Biklen, 1992; Henwood & Pidgeon, 1992; Hill, Thompson, & Williams, 1997; Stiles, 1993). CQR is a highly reliable and cost-effective method of analyzing qualitative data, making use of multiple researchers, the process of reaching consensus, and a systematic way of examining representativeness of results across cases. Once the responses to the open-ended questions are transcribed, CQR involves three steps: developing and coding domains, constructing core ideas, and developing categories to describe consistencies across cases (cross-analysis).

### ___ 5. Do the researchers state *specifically* how the method of analysis was applied?

Very satisfactory   5   4   3   2   1   Very unsatisfactory   *or*   N/A   I/I

*Comment*: The previous evaluation question suggests that the particular method of analysis should be identified and references for it should be provided. This evaluation question asks if the application of the method selected is described in sufficient detail. At a minimum, the steps followed in the analysis of the data should be described, as in Example 11.5.1. Note that the description can be quite detailed, as illustrated in Appendix D of this book.

### Example 11.5.1[10]

*Describing the steps used in the analysis of qualitative data*:

Word-for-word notes were made of participants' responses. A grounded theory

---

[9] Williams, J. K., Wyatt, G. E., Resell, J., Peterson, J., & Asuan-O'Brien, A. (2004). Psychosocial issues among gay- and non-gay-identifying HIV-seropositive African American and Latino MSM. *Cultural Diversity and Ethnic Minority Psychology, 10,* 268–286.

[10] Cockell, S. J., Zaitsoff, S. L., & Geller, J. (2004). Maintaining change following eating disorder treatment. *Professional Psychology: Research and Practice, 35,* 527–534.

approach, which involves a systematic process of indexing, coding, categorizing, and writing, was used to analyze the data (Wolcott, 1994). Specifically, Sarah J. Cockell reviewed all of the data to get a sense of the overall picture. She began by labeling each idea with a code word or phrase to capture its meaning; this served as the organizing system for the data. Codes were then grouped together on the basis of shared meaning and were arranged such that the most abstract idea in each group was labeled the *category*. She then identified the *properties* of each category (underlined in the text below)[11] and the *types, circumstances, and conditions* of each property (italicized in the text below). Shannon L. Zaitsoff and Josie Geller then reviewed this analysis. Ideas that did not fit well with the coding system were discussed, and alternative coding systems that encompassed outlying ideas were suggested. Sarah J. Cockell then reanalyzed the data, incorporating these suggestions. This process was repeated until the data were adequately captured and the coding system was supported unanimously. The final stage of analysis, which is discussed below, occurred during the writing process.

## ___ 6. Are the results of *qualitative* studies adequately supported with examples of quotations or descriptions of observations?

Very satisfactory  5  4  3  2  1  Very unsatisfactory  *or*  N/A  I/I

*Comment*: Qualitative researchers typically report few, if any, statistics in the Results section. Instead, they tend to report on what themes and categories emerged, often looking for patterns that might have implications for theory development. Instead of statistics, quotations from participants or descriptions of observations of the participants' behaviors are used to support the general statements regarding results. This is illustrated in Example 11.6.1, in which the actual words of two participants are reported to support a finding. Very often, researchers provide longer quotations that are set off in block style (i.e., indented from left and right).

### Example 11.6.1[12]
*Results of a qualitative study supported with quotations*:

The participants typically identified a career as being a lifelong endeavor, with 16 of the 18 participants expressing the view that career is a representation of lifelong goals, planning, or activity. The participants demonstrated a belief that career included a commitment, generally beyond what was necessary for a given

---

[11] The "text below" is not shown in this example. Note that the names of the individuals who conducted the analysis are given. While it is not essential, doing this is common in qualitative research but is almost never done in quantitative research reports.

[12] Juntunen, C. L. et al. (2001). American Indian perspectives on the career journey. *Journal of Counseling Psychology, 48*, 274–285.

job or type of work. In some instances, this commitment seemed to be part of the individual's self-identity. One woman responded, "It is your life" (Participant 1). Another participant discussed career as something she was born to do. "What I'm doing now, I have to do…[the Grandfather, or God] decided I will do this. I was born to do this. I will not do anything else" (Participant 13).

## ___ 7. When appropriate, are statistics reported (especially for demographic data)?

Very satisfactory  5  4  3  2  1  Very unsatisfactory  *or*  N/A  I/I

*Comment*: The main results of qualitative research are usually free of statistics. However, statistical matters often arise when writing up the results. This could be as simple as reporting the numbers of cases (whose statistical symbol is *n*). For instance, instead of reporting that "*some students* were observed with their heads down on their desks," it might be better to report that "*six students* were observed with their heads down on their desks." Too much emphasis on exact numbers, however, can be distracting in a qualitative research report. Hence, this evaluation question should be applied judiciously.

One of the most appropriate uses of statistics in qualitative research is to describe the demographics of the participants. Example 11.7.1 illustrates this.[13]

### Example 11.7.1[14]
*Demographic statistics reported in qualitative research*:

A purposive sample of 8 convicted child molesters, 7 European Americans and 1 Latino, aged 36 to 52 ($M = 44.0$, $SD = 6.4$), was recruited from an outpatient treatment facility for sex offenders in a northeastern urban community…. Four men were single; the others were either separated ($n = 2$) or divorced ($n = 2$); 3 indicated being gay or bisexual. Participants' educational levels were GED ($n = 1$), high school graduate ($n = 2$), some college ($n = 3$), some graduate work ($n = 1$), and master's degree ($n = 1$). The median annual income was $15,000–$20,000.

When there are a large number of demographic statistics, it is best to present them in a statistical table, which makes it easier for consumers of research to scan for relevant information. Example 11.7.2 shows a table of demographics presented in a qualitative research report.

---

[13] Demographic statistics are sometimes reported in the subsection on Participants in the Method section of a research report. Other times, they are reported in the Results section.
[14] Schaefer, B. M., Friedlander, M. L., Blustein, D. L., & Maruna, S. (2004). The work lives of child molesters: A phenomenological perspective. *Journal of Counseling Psychology*, *51*, 226–239.

**Example 11.7.2**[15]

*Demographic statistics in qualitative research reported in a table.*

Table 1

*Selected Participant Demographics (N = 29)*

| Demographic characteristic | Sample: Proportion (count) ($N = 29$) |
|---|---|
| Mean age in years (*SD*) | 33 (7.7) |
| Race | |
| White | 59% (17) |
| Black | 17% (5) |
| Hispanic | 17% (5) |
| Cambodian | 4% (1) |
| Missing | 0% (0) |
| Occupation | |
| Auto body repair | 3% (1) |
| Clothing sales | 3% (1) |
| Construction foreman | 7% (2) |
| Driver (truck or limo) | 17% (5) |
| Food preparation | 10% (3) |
| Mail carrier | 3% (1) |
| Manager/corporate | 17% (5) |
| Shipping/machine operations | 28% (8) |
| Teacher | 3% (1) |
| Unknown | 7% (2) |

## ___ 8. Overall, is the Results section clearly organized?

Very satisfactory   5   4   3   2   1   Very unsatisfactory   *or*   N/A   I/I

*Comment*: The Results sections of qualitative research reports are often quite long. By using subheadings throughout the Results sections, researchers can help guide their readers through sometimes complex information. Example 11.8.1 shows the major headings (in bold) and subheadings (in italics) used to help readers through a long results section of a qualitative research report.

---

[15] Rothman, E. F., & Perry, M. J. (2004). Intimate partner abuse perpetrated by employees. *Journal of Occupational Health Psychology, 9*, 238–246.

**Example 11.8.1**[16]
*Major headings (in **bold**) and subheadings (in italics) used in a long results section of a qualitative research report*:

### Results

### The Aboriginal Perspective: Cultural Factors That Serve As Barriers to Rehabilitation

> *The strength of the local and family hierarchy*
>
> *Aboriginal fatalism*

### The Non-Aboriginal Perspective: Unhelpful Stereotypes

> *Fear of Aboriginal hostility*
>
> *The self-sufficiency stereotype*
>
> *Motivational stereotypes*
>
> *The internal strife stereotype*

## ___ 9. Overall, is the presentation of the results adequate?

Very satisfactory   5   4   3   2   1   Very unsatisfactory   *or*   N/A   I/I

*Comment*: Rate this evaluation question after considering your answers to the earlier ones in this chapter and any additional considerations and concerns you may have. You may also want to raise issues based on the material in Appendix B in this book.

# Exercise for Chapter 11

## Part A

*Directions*: Answer the following questions.

1. When there are two or more individuals analyzing the data, what does "independently analyzed" mean?

2. What is the technical name of content-area experts who review preliminary research results for qualitative researchers?

---

[16] Kendall, E., & Marshall, C. A. (2004). Factors that prevent equitable access to rehabilitation for Aboriginal Australians with disabilities: The need for culturally safe rehabilitation. *Rehabilitation Psychology*, *49*, 5–13.

3. What is the name of the process by which researchers seek feedback on their preliminary results from the participants in the research?

4. The results of qualitative studies should be supported with what type of material (instead of statistics)?

5. What is one of the most appropriate uses of statistics in qualitative research?

6. Because the Results sections of qualitative research reports are often quite long, what can researchers do to help guide their readers?

## Part B

*Directions*: Locate several qualitative research reports of interest to you in academic journals.[17] Read them and evaluate the descriptions of the results in light of the evaluation questions in this chapter as well as any other considerations and concerns you may have. Select the one to which you gave the highest overall rating and bring it to class for discussion. Be prepared to discuss both its strengths and weaknesses.

---

[17] Researchers who conduct qualitative research often mention that it is qualitative in the titles or abstracts of their reports. Thus, to locate examples of qualitative research using an electronic database, it is often advantageous to use "qualitative" as a search term.

# Chapter 12

# Evaluating Discussion Sections

The last section of a research article typically has the heading "Discussion." However, expect to see variations such as "Discussion and Conclusions," "Conclusions and Implications," or "Summary and Implications."

## ___ 1. In long articles, do the researchers briefly summarize the purpose and results at the beginning of the Discussion?

Very satisfactory  5  4  3  2  1  Very unsatisfactory  *or*  N/A  I/I

*Comment*: A summary at this point in a long research article reminds readers of research of the main focus of the research and its major findings. Typically, the summary should begin by reminding readers of the main research hypotheses, purposes, or questions addressed by the research. Example 12.1.1 shows the beginning of the first paragraph of a Discussion that does this.

### Example 12.1.1[1]
*Beginning of a Discussion that reminds readers of the purpose of the research*:

The purpose of this study was to explore the way American adolescents and emerging adults from Korean, Armenian, Mexican, and European American backgrounds express autonomy and relatedness in their projected actions and reasons in response to hypothetical disagreements with parents. We examined ethnic group, age, and situational factors related to participants' actions and reasons.

The Discussion of a lengthy research report should also remind consumers of research of the main findings of the study. Complex results should be summarized in order to help consumers of research understand their main thrust. Example 12.1.2 shows a portion of such a summary of results. Note that specific statistics (previously reported in the Results sections of quantitative research reports) do not ordinarily need to be cited in such a summary.

---

[1] Phinney, J. S., Kim-Jo, T., Osorio, S., & Vilhjalmsdottir, P. (2005). Autonomy and relatedness in adolescent-parent disagreements: Ethnic and developmental factors. *Journal of Adolescent Research, 20*, 8–39.

### Example 12.1.2[2]

*Portion of a summary of results in the Discussion section of a research article*:

The most important findings are (a) participants did not increase their physical activity throughout the study, in fact, it may have decreased; (b) during the first 3 wk of the study, participants in the Feedback Condition did not increase their physical activity more than those in the No-feedback Condition; (c) during the last 3 wk of the study, there was....

## ___ 2. Do the researchers acknowledge specific methodological limitations?

Very satisfactory   5   4   3   2   1   Very unsatisfactory   *or*   N/A   I/I

*Comment*: Although the methodological limitations (i.e., weaknesses) may be discussed at any point in a research report, they are frequently included in the Discussion section because any conclusions should be drawn in light of the limitations. These are sometimes discussed under the subheading "Limitations" within the "Discussion" at the end of research reports. The two most common types of limitations are weaknesses in measurement (i.e., observation or instrumentation) and weaknesses in sampling. (See Guidelines 3 and 4 in Chapter 1.) Examples 12.2.1 and 12.2.2 show portions of descriptions of limitations that appeared in Discussion sections. Note that these limitations are important considerations in assessing the validity of the results of the studies.

### Example 12.2.1[3]

*Acknowledgment of limitations in a Discussion section*:

This study is limited by several factors. First, self-report measures in survey research are known to be error-prone, leading to conflicting or otherwise erroneous results (see Grzywacz et al. 2002). Second, although the sample was initially drawn as a random, gender-stratified sample of the...population, it is likely that some groups excluded themselves from the study by not responding. Specifically, many who do not experience success in balancing work and family may have simply been too busy and/or stressed to respond to a mailed questionnaire.

---

[2] Eastep, E. et al. (2004). Does augmented feedback from pedometers increase adults' walking behavior? *Perceptual and Motor Skills, 99,* 392–402.

[3] Clarke, M. C., Koch, L. C., & Hill, E. J. (2004). The work-family interface: Differentiating balance and fit. *Family and Consumer Sciences Research Journal, 33,* 121–140.

**Example 12.2.2**[4]

*Acknowledgment of limitations in a Discussion section*:

The use of a convenience sample and a cross-sectional design are the major limitations of the current study. The results of the current study need to be interpreted with an understanding of the impact of self-selection bias on the study sample. A convenience sample was recruited, and young women were the predominant respondents, with very few men participating. During participant recruitment, the investigator offered free BP [blood pressure] screenings for all interested persons, regardless of their willingness to participate in the actual research study. Many men would not even stop to have their BP checked.... [The trends in this study] may have been clarified if a larger number of men had participated.

## ___ 3. Are the results discussed in terms of the literature cited in the Introduction?

Very satisfactory  5  4  3  2  1  Very unsatisfactory  *or*  N/A  I/I

*Comment*: The literature cited in the Introduction sets the stage for the research. Thus, it is important to describe how the results of the research apply to the larger body of literature on the research topic. Researchers might address issues such as: Are the results consistent with those previously reported in the literature? With only some of them? With none of them? Does the study fill a gap in the literature? These are important issues to consider when drawing conclusions from a particular study. For instance, if the results of a study being evaluated are inconsistent with the results of a large number of other studies in the literature, the researcher should discuss this discrepancy and speculate on why his or her study is inconsistent with earlier ones. Examples 12.3.1 and 12.3.2 illustrate how some researchers refer to literature that is cited in the Introduction to their research reports.

**Example 12.3.1**[5]

*Discussion in terms of literature mentioned in the Introduction*:

Consistent with previous research on tobacco advertising..., this study found that patterns of storefront advertising emulate youth and adult purchasing patterns and brand preferences. Because children are also more easily influenced by images, it comes as no surprise that the brands most heavily advertised...are the most popular choices among youth.

---

[4] Peters, R. M. (2004). Racism and hypertension among African Americans. *Western Journal of Nursing Research, 26,* 612–631.
[5] Snell, C., & Bailey, L. (2005). Operation storefront: Observations of tobacco retailer advertising and compliance with tobacco laws. *Youth Violence and Juvenile Justice, 3,* 78–90.

### Example 12.3.2[6]

*Portion of a Discussion that refers to the literature mentioned in the Introduction to the research report*:

Our preliminary data indicate that early levels of distress predict psychopathology at the 6-week point. This finding is consistent with previous reports in the literature and provides some support for the notion that....

## ___ 4. Have the researchers avoided citing new references in the Discussion?

Very satisfactory  5  4  3  2  1  Very unsatisfactory  *or*  N/A  I/I

*Comment*: The relevant literature should be first cited in the Introduction. The literature referred to in the Discussion section should be limited to that originally cited in the Introduction.

## ___ 5. Are specific implications discussed?

Very satisfactory  5  4  3  2  1  Very unsatisfactory  *or*  N/A  I/I

*Comment*: Research often has implications for practicing professionals. When this is the case, a statement of implications should describe, whenever possible, specifically what a person, group, or institution should do if the results of the study are correct. Depending on the particulars of a given study, researchers may only be able to point consumers of research in a general direction as to how they might apply the results of research. In either case, it is inappropriate for researchers to assume that consumers of research will derive the implications without guidance because the implications are so obvious that they do not need discussion. Consumers of research will want to know what the researchers (who are experts on the topic) think the implications are. Example 12.5.1 is a sample statement of implications.

### Example 12.5.1[7]

*A statement of specific implications*:

An important implication for practitioners working with Latino men is that these men reflect a variety of different masculinities. The challenge for the practitioner is to use whatever broad, general information about the Latino culture is available and apply it to the circumstances of the Latino client in developing an individualized assessment and treatment modality consistent with the client's

---

[6] Resnick, H., Acierno, R., Kilpatrick, D. G., & Holmes, M. (2005). Description of an early intervention to prevent substance abuse and psychopathology in recent rape victims. *Behavior Modification, 29*, 156–188.
[7] Torres, J. B., Solberg, V. S. H., & Carlstrom, A. H. (2002). The myth of sameness among Latino men and their machismo. *American Journal of Orthopsychiatry, 72*, 163–181.

cultural gender role perspectives. Generalizations about Latinos and their diverse masculinities are not valid and may therefore present an obstacle to engaging Latino men in a therapeutic working relationship.

Reaching out to include or expand mental health services to Latinos, particularly men, requires that consideration be given to the use of nontraditional treatment approaches targeted at deconstructing or redefining those meanings embedded in the "cult of masculinity." Formats for modifying or expanding gender role perspectives relevant to Latinos may focus on providing same-gender workshops, small groups or seminars, or psychoeducational classes promoting….

## ___ 6. Are the results discussed in terms of any relevant theories?

Very satisfactory   5   4   3   2   1   Very unsatisfactory   *or*   N/A   I/l

*Comment*: As you know from earlier chapters, research that tests and/or develops theories is often important because theories provide the basis for numerous predictions and implications. If a study was introduced as theory-driven (or even clearly based on certain theoretical considerations), it is appropriate to describe how the current results affect our interpretation of the theory in the Discussion section at the end of the article. Example 12.6.1 shows a portion of such a discussion.

### Example 12.6.1[8]

*Discussion of the implications of the results of a study for theory*:

Normative theory may have fallen out of vogue in recent decades, but these findings demonstrate the value of this traditional theoretical perspective. Social norms are powerful predictors of attitudes and behaviors, and prejudice and discrimination are no exception. One advantage of the normative approach is it allows for a pragmatic optimism. Rather than facing the daunting task of changing the ingrained attitudes of millions of individuals, a norms approach suggests that changing the normative climate can be an efficient and effective approach to attitude change (see Bem, 1970). The more desirable the group, the more people will wish to follow its lead. And when people identify with attractive groups that condemn a prejudice, they are likely to win the struggle for internalization.

## ___ 7. Are suggestions for future research specific?

Very satisfactory   5   4   3   2   1   Very unsatisfactory   *or*   N/A   I/I

---

[8] Crandall, C. S., Eshleman, A., & O'Brien, L. (2002). Social norms and the expression and suppression of prejudice: The struggle for internalization. *Journal of Personality and Social Psychology, 82*, 359–378.

*Comment*: It is uninformative for researchers to conclude with a simple phrase such as "more research is needed." To be helpful, researchers should point to specific areas and research procedures that might be fruitful in future research. This is illustrated in Examples 12.7.1 and 12.7.2.

### Example 12.7.1[9]
*Specific suggestions for future research in a Discussion section*:

Future research should involve comparisons between shift workers [i.e., individuals who work nonstandard hours] and nonshift workers regarding the quality of their relationships with family members and the time spent with family and friends. Future research should include longitudinal studies in order to gain a more realistic understanding of the long-term impact of shift work on families. Moreover, quantitative and corresponding qualitative research should include family members as well as shift workers in order to determine the effects of shift work on each family participant as well as on the family unit.

### Example 12.7.2[10]
*Specific suggestions for future research*:

In sum, much more research is necessary to better understand and treat pathological gambling. First, greater knowledge of the onset and course of pathological gambling is needed. In the field of substance use disorders, early onset of use is associated with propensity to develop dependence (Hawkins et al., 1997). Because gambling initiates during or even prior to adolescence (Proimos et al., 1998), studies investigating early prevention efforts directed at high-risk populations may be useful. Numerous studies of substance abusers demonstrate an association between other psychiatric disorders and drug abuse. Similarly, for gamblers, more research is needed to assess whether affective and substance use disorders develop prior or subsequent to pathological gambling. Perhaps antidepressant treatment may be useful in the subset of gamblers whose depression preceded, rather than developed subsequent to, the gambling. Given the high rates of pathological gambling in treatment-seeking substance abusers, future studies should be directed at investigating treatments for dual diagnosis patients.

Second, better understanding of the physiology of pathological gambling also is needed. In particular, more studies characterizing withdrawal and tolerance may help inform whether medications may be useful during early stages of gambling cessation. If gambling results in physiological responses....

---

[9] Grosswald, B. (2004). The effects of shift work on family satisfaction. *Families in Society: The Journal of Contemporary Social Services, 85*, 413–423.

[10] Petry, N. M. (2002). How treatments for pathological gambling can be informed by treatments for substance use disorders. *Experimental and Clinical Psychopharmacology, 10*, 184–192.

**____ 8. Have the researchers distinguished between speculation and data-based conclusions?**

Very satisfactory  5  4  3  2  1  Very unsatisfactory  *or*  N/A  I/I

*Comment*: It is acceptable for researchers to speculate in the Discussion section (e.g., what the results might have been if the methodology had been different). However, it is important that researchers clearly distinguish between their speculation and the conclusions that can be justified by the data they have gathered. This can be done with some simple wording such as "It is interesting to speculate on the reasons for...."

**____ 9. Overall, is the Discussion effective and appropriate?**

Very satisfactory  5  4  3  2  1  Very unsatisfactory  *or*  N/A  I/I

*Comment*: Rate this evaluation question after considering your answers to the earlier ones in this chapter and any additional considerations and concerns you may have.

# Exercise for Chapter 12

**Part A**

*Directions*: Answer the following questions.

1. The methodological weaknesses of a study are sometimes discussed under what sub-heading?

2. What are the two most common types of limitations?

3. Is it ever appropriate to mention literature that was cited earlier in a research article *again* in the Discussion section at the end of a research article? Explain.

4. According to this chapter, when the implications of a study are obvious, should they be discussed anyway?

5. Suppose this was the entire suggestion for future research stated at the end of a research article: "Due to the less than definitive nature of the current research, future research is needed on the effects of negative political campaign advertisements." In your opinion, is this sufficiently specific? Explain.

6. Is it acceptable for researchers to speculate in the Discussion section of their research reports? Explain.


## Part B

*Directions*: Locate several research reports of interest to you in academic journals. Read them and evaluate the Discussion sections in light of the evaluation questions in this chapter as well as any other considerations and concerns you may have. Select the one to which you gave the highest overall rating and bring it to class for discussion. Be prepared to discuss both its strengths and weaknesses.

# Chapter 13

# Putting It All Together

If you have been faithfully applying the evaluation questions in Chapters 2 through 12, you have a series of "yes/no" answers and/or ratings from 1 to 5. Now it is time to put it all together and arrive at an overall evaluation. This should not be done mechanically, such as summing the number of times you answered "yes." Instead, an overall judgment should be made by considering the research report as a "whole." The following evaluation questions are designed to help you do this.

___ **1. In your judgment, have the researchers selected an important problem?**

Very satisfactory  5  4  3  2  1  Very unsatisfactory  *or*  N/A  I/I

*Comment*: Evaluation Question 2 in Chapter 4 asks whether the researchers have established the importance of their problem. The evaluation question being considered here is somewhat different from the one in Chapter 4 because this question asks whether *you judge* the problem to be important—even if the researcher has failed to make a strong case for its importance. In other words, a researcher may have written an Introduction that does not clearly establish the importance of the problem even though, in your judgment, it is an important one. In such a case, you would give the research report a high rating on this evaluation question but a low rating on Evaluation Question 2 in Chapter 4.

Note that a methodologically strong study on a trivial problem is a flaw that cannot be compensated for even with the best research methodology and report writing. On the other hand, a methodologically weak and poorly written study may, nevertheless, be judged to make a contribution—especially if there are no stronger studies available on the same topic, or if there are no other studies on a topic that is of great current interest.

___ **2. Were the researchers reflective?**

Very satisfactory  5  4  3  2  1  Very unsatisfactory  *or*  N/A  I/I

*Comment*: Researchers should reflect on their methodological decisions and share these reflections with their readers. This shows that careful thinking underlies their work. For example, do they reflect on why they worked with one kind of sample rather than another? Do they discuss their reasons for selecting one instrument over another for use in their research? Do they discuss their rationale for other design and procedural decisions they made in designing and conducting their research?

Researchers also should reflect on their interpretations of the data. Are there other ways to interpret the data? Are the various possible interpretations described and evaluated? Do they make it clear why they favor one interpretation over another?

Such reflections can appear throughout research reports and often are repeated in the Discussion section at the end.

## ___ 3. Is the report cohesive?

Very satisfactory  5  4  3  2  1  Very unsatisfactory  *or*  N/A  I/I

*Comment*: Do the researchers make clear the heart of the matter (usually the research hypotheses, purposes, or questions) and write a report that revolves around it and is cohesive (i.e., flows logically from one section to another)? Note that a scattered, incoherent report has little chance of making an important contribution to the understanding of a topic.

## ___ 4. Does the report extend the boundaries of our knowledge on a topic, especially our understanding of relevant theories?

Very satisfactory  5  4  3  2  1  Very unsatisfactory  *or*  N/A  I/I

*Comment*: By introducing new variables or improved methods, researchers often are able to expand our understanding of a problem. It is especially helpful when their findings provide insights into various theories or provide data that may be used for theory development. When researchers believe their data clearly extend the boundaries of what we know about a research problem, they should state that they believe this is the case. Example 13.4.1 is from the Introduction to a research report. The researchers state that their research has the potential to extend the boundaries of knowledge.

### Example 13.4.1[1]

*Researchers state in the Introduction that their study will extend knowledge of the topic [bold added for emphasis]:*

There is a strong rationale for the development of interventions to assist with memory problems in early-stage Alzheimer's Disease (AD). Despite severe episodic memory impairment, some components of memory are relatively preserved (Brandt & Rich, 1995), and a continued capacity for learning means that,

---

[1] Clare, L., Wilson, B. A., Carter, G., Roth, I., & Hodges, J. R. (2002). Relearning face–name associations in early Alzheimer's Disease. *Neuropsychology, 16,* 538–547.

given appropriate cognitive support (Bäckman, 1992), memory performance can be facilitated. This effect is evident both in relation to procedural (Zanetti et al., 1997, 2001) and verbal (Camp, Bird, & Cherry, 2000) memory tasks. A recent review of empirically validated treatments for older people (Gatz et al., 1998) classified "memory therapy" as "probably efficacious," indicating that it has some promise and that further research is warranted to **extend the evidence base and clarify outstanding questions.**

Example 13.4.2 is excerpted from the Discussion section of a research report in which the researchers state that their findings replicate and extend what is known about an issue. Note in footnote 2 that the title of the article from which the example was drawn uses the term "extension."

### Example 13.4.2[2]

*Researchers state in the Discussion section that their study extended knowledge of the topic [bold added for emphasis]:*

The present findings must be replicated in future studies using more naturalistic tasks in nonlaboratory settings or with other behavioral assessments. However, it should be noted that the present finding of lack of Asian–White differences on behavioral indexes during a social performance task **replicates and extends the past findings** of verbal assertion with Chinese Americans using simulated role plays (D. Sue et al., 1983, 1990).

Example 13.4.3 is excerpted from the Discussion section of a research report in which the researchers note that their results provide support for a theory.

### Example 13.4.3[3]

*Researchers state in the Discussion section that their study helps to support a theory [bold added for emphasis]:*

In general, **the results provide support for Hobfoll's conservation of resources theory** (Hobfoll, 1989, 2001) as a general framework to understand role strain in low-income women. On the basis of this theory, we postulated that factors conceptualized as resources would be associated with lower levels of role strain, whereas characteristics that could potentially drain resources would be associated with higher levels of strain. Our results provide partial support for our hypotheses, particularly in the realms of family and work characteristics. For example, the number of young children, having children with impulsive and difficult temperaments, having children with disabilities, and lacking child care all

---

[2] Okazaki, S., Liu, J. F., Longworth, S. L., & Minn, J. Y. (2002). Asian American–White American differences in expressions of social anxiety: A replication and extension. *Cultural Diversity and Ethnic Minority Psychology, 8,* 234–247.

[3] Morris, J. E., & Coley, R. L. (2004). Maternal, family, and work correlates of role strain in low-income mothers. *Journal of Family Psychology, 18,* 424–432.

related to higher levels of maternal role strain. These characteristics are likely to deplete maternal resources....

In some cases, a researcher may fail to point out that his or her research extends what we know, but *you may judge* that the research does extend it and give the research a satisfactory rating on this evaluation question. In other words, this evaluation question asks only whether the research extends what we know—not whether the researcher establishes that it does so.

## ___ 5. Are any major methodological flaws unavoidable or forgivable?

Very satisfactory  5  4  3  2  1  Very unsatisfactory  *or*  N/A  I/I

*Comment*: No study is perfect, but some are more seriously flawed than others. When serious flaws are encountered, consider whether they were unavoidable. For example, obtaining a random sample of street prostitutes for a study on AIDS transmission is probably impossible. However, if the researchers went to the trouble to contact them at different times of the day in various locations (not just the safer parts of a city) and obtained a high rate of participation from those who were contacted, the failure to obtain a random sample would be forgivable because the flaw was unavoidable and considerable effort was made to contact more than just a convenient group of participants. Contrast this with researchers who want to generalize from a sample of fourth graders to a larger population but simply settle for a classroom of students who are readily accessible because they attend the university's demonstration school on the university campus. The failure to use random sampling, or at least get a more diverse sample, is not unavoidable and should be counted as a serious flaw.

Unless some flaws under some circumstances are tolerated, the vast majority of research in the social and behavioral sciences would need to be summarily rejected. Instead, as a practical matter, we tolerate certain flaws but interpret the data from seriously flawed studies with considerable caution.

## ___ 6. Is the research likely to inspire additional research?

Very satisfactory  5  4  3  2  1  Very unsatisfactory  *or*  N/A  I/I

*Comment*: Even if a study is seriously flawed, it can receive a high evaluation on this question if it is likely to inspire others to study the problem. Seriously flawed research is most likely to get high ratings on this evaluation question if it has surprising findings or helps to advance the development of a theory. Keep in mind that research on a problem is an ongoing *process*, with each study contributing to the base of knowledge about a topic. A study that stimulates the process and moves it forward is worthy of our attention—even if it is seriously flawed or is only a pilot study.

**\_\_\_ 7. Is the research likely to help in decision making?**

Very satisfactory  5  4  3  2  1  Very unsatisfactory  *or*  N/A  I/I

*Comment*: Even seriously flawed research sometimes can help decision makers. Suppose a researcher conducted an experiment on a new drug-resistance educational program with no control group (usually considered a serious flaw) and found that students' illicit drug usage actually went up from pretest to posttest. Such a finding might lead to the decision to abandon the educational program, especially if other studies with different types of flaws produced results consistent with this one.

When applying this evaluation question, consider how comfortable you would be making an important decision based on the study you are evaluating. In the absence of any other studies on the same topic, would this study help you make a more informed decision than if the study did not exist?

**\_\_\_ 8. All things considered, is the report worthy of publication in an academic journal?**

Very satisfactory  5  4  3  2  1  Very unsatisfactory  *or*  N/A  I/I

*Comment*: Given that space is limited in academic journals, with some journals rejecting more than 90% of the research reports submitted, is the report you are evaluating worthy of publication?

**\_\_\_ 9. Would you be proud to have your name on the research article as a co-author?**

Very satisfactory  5  4  3  2  1  Very unsatisfactory  *or*  N/A  I/I

*Comment*: This is the most subjective evaluation question in this book, and it is fitting that it is last. Would you want to be personally associated with the research you are evaluating?

# Concluding Comment

I hope that as a result of reading and working through this book, you have become a critical consumer of research while recognizing that conducting solid research in the social and behavioral sciences is often difficult (and conducting "perfect research" is impossible).

Note that the typical research methods textbook attempts to show *what should be done in the ideal*. Textbook authors do this because their usual purpose is to train students in how to conduct research. Unless a student knows what the ideal standards for research are, he or she is likely to fall unintentionally into many traps. However, when evaluating reports of research in academic journals, it is unreasonable to hold each article up to ideal "textbook standards." Researchers conduct research under less-than-ideal conditions, usually with limited resources. In addition, they typically are forced to make many compromises (especially in measurement and sampling) given the practical realities of typical research settings. A fair and meaningful evaluation of a research article takes these matters into consideration.

# Appendix A[1]

# Quantitative and Qualitative Research: An Overview

Because *quantitative* researchers reduce information to statistics such as averages, percentages, and so on, their research reports are easy to spot. If a report has a Results section devoted mainly to the presentation of statistical data, it is a report of quantitative research. This approach to research dominated the social and behavioral sciences throughout most of the 1900s and still represents the majority of published research in the 2000s. Thus, for most topics, you are likely to locate many more articles reporting quantitative research than qualitative research.

In the ideal, those who conduct *quantitative research* should do the following:

1. Start with one or more very specific, explicitly stated research hypotheses, purposes, or questions, ideally derived from theory and/or previous research. They make research plans that focus narrowly on the stated hypotheses, purposes, or questions (as opposed to being wide ranging and exploratory).

2. Select a random sample (like drawing names out of a hat) from a population so that the sample is representative of the population from which it was drawn.[2]

3. Use a relatively large sample of participants, sometimes as many as 1,500 for a national survey. Some quantitative researchers use even larger samples, but many use much smaller ones because of limited resources. A study with a large sample is usually a quantitative one.

4. Make observations with instruments that can be scored objectively, such as multiple-choice achievement tests and attitude scales in which participants mark choices such as "strongly agree" to "strongly disagree."

5. Describe results using statistics, and make inferences to the population from which the sample was drawn (i.e., inferring that what the researcher found by studying a sample is similar to what he or she would have found by studying the entire population from which the sample was drawn).

---

[1] This appendix is based in part on material drawn with permission from Galvan, J. L. (2004). *Writing literature reviews: A guide for students of the social and behavioral sciences* (2nd ed.). Glendale, CA: Pyrczak Publishing. Copyright ©2004 by Pyrczak Publishing. All rights reserved.

[2] It is "representative" except for the effects of random errors, which can be assessed with inferential statistics. Chapter 7 points out that researchers do not always sample or need random samples.

In addition, quantitative research is characterized by "distance" between researchers and their participants. That is, quantitative researchers typically have limited contact with their participants. In fact, it is not uncommon for the researcher to have no direct contact with them. For instance, a quantitative researcher might have teachers administer tests to students without ever seeing or talking with the students. Even if the researcher is physically present in the research setting, he or she usually follows a prearranged script for the study and avoids unplanned personal interactions.

*Qualitative research* also has a long tradition in the social and behavioral sciences, but has gained a large following in many applied fields only in recent decades. It also is often easy to identify because the titles of the articles frequently contain the word "qualitative." In addition, qualitative researchers usually identify their research as qualitative in their Introductions as well as in other parts of their reports.[3] You can also identify qualitative research because the Results section will be presented in terms of a narrative describing themes and trends, which are very often illustrated with quotations from the participants.

In the ideal, those who conduct *qualitative research* should do the following:

1. Start with a general research question or problem, and *not* formulate hypotheses derived from previously published literature or theories. Although qualitative researchers avoid starting with hypotheses and theories, they may emerge (i.e., a qualitative researcher may formulate hypotheses or theories that explain his or her observations) while conducting the research. Such hypotheses and theories are subject to change as additional data are collected during the study. Thus, there is a fluid interaction between the data collection, data analysis, and any hypotheses or theories that may emerge.

2. Select a purposive sample—not a random one. A purposive sample is one in which the researcher has some special research interest and is not necessarily representative of a larger population. In other words, the researcher intentionally draws what he or she believes to be an appropriate sample for the research problem, without regard to random selection.

3. Use a relatively small sample—sometimes as small as one exemplary case, but more often small groups of people or units such as classrooms, churches, and so on.

4. Observe with relatively unstructured instruments such as semistructured interviews, unstructured direct observations, and so on.

5. Observe intensively (e.g., spending extended periods of time with the participants to gain in-depth insights into the phenomena of interest).

---

[3] Note that quantitative researchers rarely explicitly state that their research is quantitative. Because the overwhelming majority of research reports in journals is quantitative, readers will assume that it is quantitative unless told otherwise.

6. Present results mainly or exclusively in words, with an emphasis on understanding the particular purposive sample studied and a de-emphasis on making generalizations to larger populations.

In addition, qualitative research is characterized by the researchers' awareness of their own orientations, biases, and experiences that might affect their collection and interpretation of data. It is not uncommon for qualitative researchers to include in their research reports a statement on these issues and what steps they took to see beyond their own subjective experiences in order to understand their research problems from the participants' points of view. Thus, there is a tendency for qualitative research to be personal and interactive. This is in contrast to quantitative research, in which researchers attempt to be objective and distant.

As you can see from the above, the fact that the two research traditions are quite distinct will need to be taken into account when evaluating research reports. Those of you who are just beginning to learn about qualitative research are urged to read Appendix B in this book, which discusses some important issues in its evaluation.

*Notes*:

# Appendix B

# Examining the Validity Structure of Qualitative Research

R. BURKE JOHNSON
University of South Alabama

ABSTRACT. Three types of validity in qualitative research are discussed. First, descriptive validity refers to the factual accuracy of the account as reported by the qualitative researcher. Second, interpretive validity is obtained to the degree that the participants' viewpoints, thoughts, intentions, and experiences are accurately understood and reported by the qualitative researcher. Third, theoretical validity is obtained to the degree that a theory or theoretical explanation developed from a research study fits the data and is, therefore, credible and defensible. The two types of validity that are typical of quantitative research, internal and external validity, are also discussed for qualitative research. Twelve strategies used to promote research validity in qualitative research are discussed.

From *Education*, *118*, 282–292. Copyright © 1997 by Project Innovation. Reprinted with permission of the publisher and author.

Discussions of the term "validity" have traditionally been attached to the quantitative research tradition. Not surprisingly, reactions by qualitative researchers have been mixed regarding whether or not this concept should be applied to qualitative research. At the extreme, some qualitative researchers have suggested that the traditional quantitative criteria of reliability and validity are not relevant to qualitative research (e.g., Smith, 1984). Smith contends that the basic epistemological and ontological assumptions of quantitative and qualitative research are incompatible, and, therefore, the concepts of reliability and validity should be abandoned. Most qualitative researchers, however, probably hold a more moderate viewpoint. Most qualitative researchers argue that some qualitative

research studies are better than others, and they frequently use the term validity to refer to this difference. When qualitative researchers speak of research validity, they are usually referring to qualitative research that is plausible, credible, trustworthy, and, therefore, defensible. We believe it is important to think about the issue of validity in qualitative research and to examine some strategies that have been developed to maximize validity (Kirk & Miller, 1986; LeCompte & Preissle, 1993; Lincoln & Guba, 1985; Maxwell, 1996). A list of these strategies is provided in Table 1.

One potential threat to validity that researchers must be careful to watch out for is called *researcher bias*. This problem is summed up in a statement a colleague of mine once made to me. She said, "The problem with qualitative research is that the researchers find what they want to find, and then they write up their results." It is true that the problem of researcher bias is frequently an issue because qualitative research is open-ended and less structured than quantitative research. This is because qualitative research tends to be exploratory. (One would be remiss, however, to think that researcher bias is never a problem in quantitative research!) Researcher bias tends to result from selective observation and selective recording of information, and also from allowing one's personal views and perspectives to affect how data are interpreted and how the research is conducted.

The key strategy used to understand researcher bias is called *reflexivity*, which means that the researcher actively engages in critical self-reflection about his or her potential biases and predispositions (Table 1). Through reflexivity, researchers become more self-aware, and they monitor and

Table 1
*Strategies Used to Promote Qualitative Research Validity*

| Strategy | Description |
| --- | --- |
| Researcher as "detective" | A metaphor characterizing the qualitative researcher as he or she searches for evidence about causes and effects. The researcher develops an understanding of the data through careful consideration of potential causes and effects and by systematically eliminating "rival" explanations or hypotheses until the final "case" is made "beyond a reasonable doubt." The "detective" can utilize any of the strategies listed here. |
| Extended fieldwork | When possible, qualitative researchers should collect data in the field over an extended period of time. |
| Low inference descriptors | The use of description phrased very close to the participants' accounts and researchers' field notes. Verbatims (i.e., direct quotations) are a commonly used type of low inference descriptors. |
| Triangulation | "Cross-checking" information and conclusions through the use of multiple procedures or sources. When the different procedures or sources are in agreement, you have "corroboration." |
| Data triangulation | The use of multiple data sources to help understand a phenomenon. |
| Methods triangulation | The use of multiple research methods to study a phenomenon. |
| Investigator triangulation | The use of multiple investigators (i.e., multiple researchers) in collecting and interpreting the data. |
| Theory triangulation | The use of multiple theories and perspectives to help interpret and explain the data. |
| Participant feedback | The feedback and discussion of the researcher's interpretations and conclusions with the actual participants and other members of the participant community for verification and insight. |
| Peer review | Discussion of the researcher's interpretations and conclusions with other people. This includes discussion with a "disinterested peer" (e.g., with another researcher not directly involved). This peer should be skeptical and play the "devil's advocate," challenging the researcher to provide solid evidence for any interpretations or conclusions. Discussion with peers who are familiar with the research can also help provide useful challenges and insights. |
| Negative case sampling | Locating and examining cases that disconfirm the researcher's expectations and tentative explanation. |
| Reflexivity | This involves self-awareness and "critical self-reflection" by the researcher on his or her potential biases and predispositions as these may affect the research process and conclusions. |
| Pattern matching | Predicting a series of results that form a "pattern" and then determining the degree to which the actual results fit the predicted pattern. |

attempt to control their biases. Many qualitative researchers include a distinct section in their research proposals titled Researcher Bias. In this section, they discuss their personal background, how it may affect their research, and what strategies they will use to address the potential problem. Another strategy that qualitative researchers use to reduce the effect of researcher bias is called *negative case sampling* (Table 1). This means that they attempt carefully and purposively to search for examples that disconfirm their expectations and explanations about what they are studying. If you use this approach, you will find it more difficult to ignore important information, and you will come up with more credible and defensible results.

We will now examine some types of validity that are important in qualitative research. We will start with three types of validity that are especially relevant to qualitative research (Maxwell, 1992, 1996). These types are called descriptive validity, interpretive validity, and theoretical validity. They are important to qualitative research because description of what is observed and interpretation of participants' thoughts are two primary qualitative research activities. For example, ethnography produces descriptions and accounts of the lives and experiences of groups of people with a focus on cultural characteristics (Fetterman, 1998; LeCompte & Preissle, 1993). Ethnographers also attempt to understand groups of people from the insider's perspective (i.e., from the viewpoints of the people in the group; called the *emic* perspective). Developing a theoretical explanation of the behavior of group members is also of interest to qualitative researchers, especially qualitative researchers using the grounded theory perspective (Glaser & Strauss, 1967; Strauss & Corbin, 1990). After discussing these three forms of validity, the traditional types of validity used in quantitative research, internal and external validity, are discussed. Internal validity is relevant when qualitative researchers explore cause and effect relationships. External validity is relevant when qualitative researchers generalize beyond their research studies.

### Descriptive Validity

The first type of validity in qualitative research is called *descriptive validity*. Descriptive validity refers to the factual accuracy of the account as reported by the researchers. The key questions addressed in descriptive validity are: Did what was reported as taking place in the group being studied actually happen? and Did the researchers accurately report what they saw and heard? In other words, descriptive validity refers to accuracy in reporting descriptive information (e.g., description of events, objects, behaviors, people, settings, times, and places). This form of validity is important because description is a major objective in nearly all qualitative research.

One effective strategy used to obtain descriptive validity is called *investigator triangulation*. In the case of descriptive validity, investigator triangulation involves the use of multiple observers to record and describe the research participants' behavior and the context in which they were located. The use of multiple observers allows cross-checking of observations to make sure the investigators agree about what took place. When corroboration (i.e., agreement) of observations across multiple investigators is obtained, it is less likely that outside reviewers of the research will question whether something occurred. As a result, the research will be more credible and defensible.

### Interpretive Validity

While descriptive validity refers to accuracy in reporting the facts, interpretive validity requires developing a window into the minds of the people being studied. *Interpretive validity* refers to accurately portraying the *meaning* attached by participants to what is being studied by the researcher. More specifically, it refers to the degree to which the research participants' viewpoints, thoughts, feelings, intentions, and experiences are accurately

understood by the qualitative researcher and portrayed in the research report. An important part of qualitative research is understanding research participants' inner worlds (i.e., their phenomenological worlds), and interpretive validity refers to the degree of accuracy in presenting these inner worlds. Accurate interpretive validity requires that the researcher gets inside the heads of the participants, looks through the participants' eyes, and sees and feels what they see and feel. In this way, the qualitative researcher can understand things from the participants' perspectives and provide a valid account of these perspectives.

Some strategies for achieving interpretive validity are provided in Table 1. *Participant feedback* is perhaps the most important strategy (Table 1). This strategy has also been called "member checking" (Lincoln & Guba, 1985). By sharing your interpretations of participants' viewpoints with the participants and other members of the group, you may clear up areas of miscommunication. Do the people being studied agree with what you have said about them? While this strategy is not perfect because some participants may attempt to put on a good face, useful information is frequently obtained and inaccuracies are often identified.

When writing the research report, using many low inference descriptors is also helpful so that the reader can experience the participants' actual language, dialect, and personal meanings (Table 1). A verbatim is the lowest inference descriptor of all because the participants' exact words are provided in direct quotations. Here is an example of a verbatim from a high school dropout who was part of an ethnographic study of high school dropouts:

> I wouldn't do the work. I didn't like the teacher and I didn't like my mom and dad. So, even if I did my work, I wouldn't turn it in. I completed it. I just didn't want to turn it in. I was angry with my mom and dad because they were talking about moving out of state at the time (Okey & Cusick, 1995: p. 257).

This verbatim provides some description (i.e., what the participant did) but it also provides some information about the participant's interpretations and personal meanings (which is the topic of interpretive validity). The participant expresses his frustration and anger toward his parents and teacher, and shares with us what homework meant to him at the time and why he acted as he did. By reading verbatims like this one, readers of a report can experience for themselves the participants' perspectives. Again, getting into the minds of research participants is a common goal in qualitative research, and Maxwell calls our accuracy in portraying this inner content interpretive validity.

## Theoretical Validity

The third type of validity in qualitative research is called *theoretical validity*. You have theoretical validity to the degree that a theoretical explanation developed from a research study fits the data and, therefore, is credible and defensible. Theory usually refers to discussions of *how* a phenomenon operates and *why* it operates as it does. Theory is usually more abstract and less concrete than description and interpretation. Theory development moves beyond just the facts and provides an explanation of the phenomenon. In the words of Joseph Maxwell (1992):

> One could label the student's throwing of the eraser as an act of resistance, and connect this act to the repressive behavior or values of the teacher, the social structure of the school, and class relationships in U.S. society. The identification of the throwing as resistance constitutes the application of a theoretical construct...the connection of this to other aspects of the participants, the school, or the community constitutes the postulation of theoretical relationships among these constructs (p. 291).

In the above example, the theoretical construct called "resistance" is used to explain the student's behavior. Maxwell points out that the construct of resistance may also be related to other theoretical constructs or variables. In fact, theories are often developed by relating theoretical constructs.

A strategy for promoting theoretical validity is *extended fieldwork* (Table 1). This means that you should spend a sufficient amount of time studying your research participants and their setting so that you can have confidence that the patterns of relationships you believe are operating are stable and so that you can understand why these relationships occur. As you spend more time in the field collecting data and generating and testing your inductive hypotheses, your theoretical explanation may become more detailed and intricate. You may also decide to use the strategy called *theory triangulation* (Table 1; Denzin, 1989). This means that you would examine how the phenomenon being studied would be explained by different theories. The various theories might provide you with insights and help you develop a more cogent explanation.

In a related way, you might also use investigator triangulation and consider the ideas and explanations generated by additional researchers studying the research participants.

As you develop your theoretical explanation, you should make some predictions based on the theory and test the accuracy of those predictions. When doing this, you can use the *pattern matching* strategy (Table 1). In pattern matching, the strategy is to make several predictions at once; then, if all of the predictions occur as predicted (i.e., if the pattern is found), you have evidence supporting your explanation. As you develop your theoretical explanation, you should also use the negative case sampling strategy mentioned earlier (Table 1). That is, you must always search for cases or examples that do not fit your explanation so that you do not simply find the data that support your developing theory. As a general rule, your final explanation should accurately reflect the majority of the people in your research study. Another useful strategy for promoting theoretical validity is called *peer review* (Table 1). This means that you should try to spend some time discussing your explanation with your colleagues so that they can search for problems with it. Each problem must then be resolved. In some cases, you will find that you will need to go back to the field and collect additional data. Finally, when developing a theoretical explanation, you must also think about the issues of internal validity and external validity, to which we now turn.

## Internal Validity

Internal validity is the fourth type of validity in qualitative research of interest to us. Internal validity refers to the degree to which a researcher is justified in concluding that an observed relationship is causal (Cook & Campbell, 1979). Often, qualitative researchers are not interested in cause-and-effect relationships. Sometimes, however, qualitative researchers are interested in identifying potential causes and effects. In fact, qualitative research can be very helpful in describing how phenomena operate (i.e., studying process) and in developing and testing preliminary causal hypotheses and theories (Campbell, 1979; Johnson, 1994; LeCompte & Preissle, 1993; Strauss, 1995; 1994).

When qualitative researchers identify potential cause-and-effect relationships, they must think about many of the same issues that quantitative researchers must consider. They should also think about the strategies used for obtaining theoretical validity discussed earlier. The qualitative researcher takes on the role of the detective searching for the true cause(s) of a phenomenon, examining each possible clue, and attempting to rule out each rival explanation generated (see *researcher as "detective"* in Table 1). When trying to identify a causal relationship, the researcher makes mental comparisons. The comparison might be to a hypothetical control group. Although a control group is rarely used in qualitative research, the researcher can think about what would have happened if the causal factor had not occurred. The researcher can sometimes rely on his or her expert opinion, as well as published research studies when available, in deciding what would have happened. Furthermore, if the event is something that occurs again, the researcher can determine if the causal factor precedes the outcome. In other words, when the causal factor occurs again, does the effect follow?

When a researcher believes that an observed relationship is causal, he or she must also attempt to make sure that the observed change in the dependent variable is due to the independent variable and not to something else (e.g., a confounding extraneous variable). The successful researcher will always make a list of rival explanations or rival hypotheses, which are possible or plausible reasons for the relationship other than the originally suspected cause. Be creative and think of as many rival explanations as you can. One way to get started is to be a skeptic and think of reasons why the relationship should not be causal. Each rival explanation must be examined after the list has been developed. Sometimes you will be able to check a rival explanation with the data you have already collected through additional data analysis. At other times you will need to collect additional data. One strategy would be to observe the relationship you believe to be causal under conditions where the confounding variable is not present and compare this outcome with the original outcome. For example, if you concluded that a teacher effectively maintained classroom discipline on a given day but a critic maintained that it was the result of a parent visiting the classroom on that day, then you should try to observe the teacher again when the parent is not present. If the teacher is still successful, you have some evidence that the original

finding was not because of the presence of the parent in the classroom.

All of the strategies shown in Table 1 are used to improve the internal validity of qualitative research. Now we will explain the only two strategies not yet discussed (i.e., methods triangulation and data triangulation). When using *methods triangulation*, the researcher uses more than one method of research in a single research study. The word methods should be used broadly here, and it refers to different methods of research (e.g., ethnography, survey, experimental, etc.) as well as to different types of data collection procedures (e.g., interviews, questionnaires, and observations). You can intermix any of these (e.g., ethnography and survey research methods, or interviews and observations, or experimental research and interviews). The logic is to combine different methods that have "nonoverlapping weaknesses and strengths" (Brewer & Hunter, 1989). The weaknesses (and strengths) of one method will tend to be different from those of a different method, which means that when you combine two or more methods, you will have better evidence! In other words, the "whole" is better than its "parts."

Here is an example of methods triangulation. Perhaps you are interested in why students in an elementary classroom stigmatize a certain student named Brian. A stigmatized student would be an individual that is not well liked, has a lower status, and is seen as different from the normal students. Perhaps Brian has a different haircut from the other students, is dressed differently, or doesn't act like the other students. In this case, you might decide to observe how students treat Brian in various situations. In addition to observing the students, you will probably decide to interview Brian and the other students to understand their beliefs and feelings about Brian. A strength of observational data is that you can actually see the students' behaviors. A weakness of interviews is that what the students say and what they actually do may be different. However, using interviews you can delve into the students' thinking and reasoning, whereas you cannot do this using observational data. Therefore, the whole will likely be better than the parts.

When using *data triangulation*, the researcher uses multiple data sources in a single research study. "Data sources" does not mean using different methods. Data triangulation refers to the use of multiple data sources using a single method. For example, the use of multiple interviews would provide multiple data sources while using a single method (i.e., the interview method). Likewise, the use of multiple observations would be another example of data triangulation; multiple data sources would be provided while using a single method (i.e., the observational method). Another important part of data triangulation involves collecting data at different times, at different places, and with different people.

Here is an example of data triangulation. Perhaps a researcher is interested in studying why certain students are apathetic. It would make sense to get the perspectives of several different kinds of people. The researcher might interview teachers, interview students identified by the teachers as being apathetic, and interview peers of apathetic students. Then the researcher could check to see if the information obtained from these different data sources was in agreement. Each data source may provide additional reasons as well as a different perspective on the question of student apathy, resulting in a more complete understanding of the phenomenon. The researcher should also interview apathetic students at different class periods during the day and in different types of classes (e.g., math and social studies). Through the rich information gathered (e.g., from different people, at different times, and at different places) the researcher can develop a better understanding of why students are apathetic than if only one data source is used.

### External Validity

External validity is important when you want to generalize from a set of research findings to other people, settings, and times (Cook & Campbell, 1979). Typically, generalizability is not the major purpose of qualitative research. There are at least two reasons for this. First, the people and settings examined in qualitative research are rarely randomly selected, and, as you know, random selection is the best way to generalize from a sample to a population. As a result, qualitative research is virtually always weak in the form of population validity focused on "generalizing to populations" (i.e., generalizing from a sample to a population).

Second, some qualitative researchers are more interested in documenting particularistic findings than universalistic findings. In other words, in certain forms of qualitative research the goal is to show what is unique about a certain group of peo-

ple, or a certain event, rather than generate findings that are broadly applicable. At a fundamental level, many qualitative researchers do not believe in the presence of general laws or universal laws. General laws are things that apply to many people, and universal laws are things that apply to everyone. As a result, qualitative research is frequently considered weak on the "generalizing across populations" form of population validity (i.e., generalizing to different kinds of people), and on ecological validity (i.e., generalizing across settings) and temporal validity (i.e., generalizing across times).

Other experts argue that rough generalizations can be made from qualitative research. Perhaps the most reasonable stance toward the issue of generalizing is that we can generalize to other people, settings, and times to the degree that they are similar to the people, settings, and times in the original study. Stake (1990) uses the term *naturalistic generalization*[1] to refer to this process of generalizing based on similarity. The bottom line is this: The more similar the people and circumstances in a particular research study are to the ones that you want to generalize to, the more defensible your generalization will be and the more readily you should make such a generalization.

To help readers of a research report know when they can generalize, qualitative researchers should provide the following kinds of information: the number and kinds of people in the study, how they were selected to be in the study, contextual information, the nature of the researcher's relationship with the participants, information about any informants who provided information, the methods of data collection used, and the data analysis techniques used. This information is usually reported in the Methodology section of the final research report. Using the information included in a well-written Methodology section, readers will be able to make informed decisions about to whom the results may be generalized. They will also have the information they will need if they decide to replicate the research study with new participants.

Some experts show another way to generalize

---

[1] Donald Campbell (1986) makes a similar point, and he uses the term *proximal similarity* to refer to the degree of similarity between the people and circumstances in the original research study and the people and circumstances to which you wish to apply the findings. Using Campbell's term, your goal is to check for proximal similarity.

from qualitative research (e.g., Yin, 1994). Qualitative researchers can sometimes use *replication logic,* just like the replication logic that is commonly used by experimental researchers when they generalize beyond the people in their studies, even when they do not have random samples. According to replication logic, the more times a research finding is shown to be true with different sets of people, the more confidence we can place in the finding and in the conclusion that the finding generalizes beyond the people in the original research study (Cook & Campbell, 1979). In other words, if the finding is replicated with different kinds of people and in different places, then the evidence may suggest that the finding applies very broadly. Yin's key point is that there is no reason why replication logic cannot be applied to certain kinds of qualitative research.[2]

Here is an example. Over the years you may observe a certain pattern of relations between boys and girls in your third-grade classroom. Now assume that you decided to conduct a qualitative research study and you find that the pattern of relation occurred in your classroom and in two other third-grade classrooms you studied. Because your research is interesting, you decide to publish it. Then other researchers replicate your study with other people and they find that the same relationship holds in the third-grade classrooms they studied. According to replication logic, the more times a theory or a research finding is replicated with other people, the greater the support for the theory or research finding. Now assume further that other researchers find that the relationship holds in classrooms at several other grade levels (e.g., first grade, second grade, fourth grade, and fifth grade). If this happens, the evidence suggests that the finding generalizes to students in other grade levels, adding additional generality to the finding.

One more comment before concluding: If generalizing through replication and theoretical validity (discussed above) sound similar, that is because they are. Basically, generalizing (i.e., external validity) is frequently part of theoretical validity. In other words, when researchers develop theoretical explanations, they often want to generalize beyond their original research study. Likewise, internal validity is also important for theoretical validity if cause and effect statements are made.

## References

Brewer, J., & Hunter, A. (1989). *Multimethod research: A synthesis of styles.* Newbury Park, CA: Sage.

Campbell, D. T. (1979). Degrees of freedom and the case study. In T. D. Cook & C. S. Reichardt (Eds.), *Qualitative and quantitative methods in evaluation research* (pp. 49–67). Beverly Hills, CA: Sage Publications.

Campbell, D. T. (1986). Relabeling internal and external validity for applied social scientists. In W. Trochim (Ed.), *Advances in quasi-experimental design and analysis: New directions for program evaluation, 31,* San Francisco: Jossey-Bass.

Cook, T. D., & Campbell, D. T. (1979). *Quasi-experimentation: Design and analysis issues for field settings.* Chicago: Rand McNally.

Denzin, N. K. (1989). *The research act: Theoretical introduction to sociological methods.* Englewood Cliffs, NJ: Prentice Hall.

Fetterman, D. M. (1998). Ethnography. In *Handbook of Applied Social Research Methods* by L. Bickman & D. J. Rog (Eds.). Thousand Oaks, CA: Sage.

Glaser, B. G., & Strauss, A. L. (1967). *The discovery of grounded theory: Strategies for qualitative research.* New York: Aldine de Gruyter.

Johnson, R. B. (1994). Qualitative research in education. *SRATE Journal, 4*(1), 3–7.

Kirk, J., & Miller, M. L. (1986). *Reliability and validity in qualitative research.* Newbury Park, CA: Sage.

LeCompte, M. D., & Preissle, J. (1993). *Ethnography and qualitative design in educational research.* San Diego, CA: Academic Press.

Lincoln, Y. S., & Guba, E. G. (1985). *Naturalistic inquiry.* Beverly Hills, CA: Sage.

Maxwell, J. A. (1992). Understanding and validity in qualitative research. *Harvard Educational Review, 62*(3), 279–299.

Maxwell, J. A. (1996). *Qualitative research design.* Newbury Park, CA: Sage.

Okey, T. N., & Cusick, P. A. (1995). Dropping out: Another side of the story. *Educational Administration Quarterly, 31*(2), 244–267.

Smith, J. K. (1984). The problem of criteria for judging interpretive inquiry. *Educational Evaluation and Policy Analysis, 6,* 379–391.

Stake, R. E. (1990). Situational context as influence on evaluation design and use. *Studies in Educational Evaluation, 16,* 231–246.

Strauss, A. (1995). Notes on the nature and development of general theories. *Qualitative Inquiry 1*(1), 7–18.

Strauss, A., & Corbin, J. (1990). *Basics of qualitative research: Grounded theory procedures and techniques.* Newbury Park, CA: Sage.

Yin, R. K. (1994). *Case study research: Design and methods.* Newbury Park: Sage.

---

[2] The late Donald Campbell, perhaps the most important quantitative research methodologist over the past 50 years, approved of Yin's (1994) book. See, for example, his Introduction to that book.

*Notes*:

# Appendix C

# The Limitations of Significance Testing

Most of the quantitative research you evaluate will contain significance tests. They are important tools for quantitative researchers but have two major limitations. Before discussing the limitations, consider the purpose of significance testing and the types of information it provides.

*The Function of Significance Testing*

The function of significance testing is to help researchers evaluate the role of chance errors due to sampling. Statisticians refer to these chance errors as *sampling errors*. As you will see later in this appendix, it is very important to note that the term *sampling errors* is statistical jargon that refers only to *chance* errors. Where do these sampling errors come from? They result from random sampling. Random sampling (e.g., drawing names out of a hat) gives everyone in a population an equal chance of being selected. Random sampling also produces random errors (once again, known as *sampling errors*). Consider Examples C.1 and C.2 to get a better understanding of this problem. Note in Example C.1 that when whole populations are tested, there are no sampling errors and, hence, significance tests are not needed. It is also important to note in this example that *a real difference can be a small difference* (in this example, less than a full point on a 30-item test).

**Example C.1**

*Example with no sampling errors because a whole population of tenth graders was tested*:

A team of researchers tested all 500 tenth graders in a school district with a highly reliable and valid current events test consisting of 30 multiple-choice items. The team obtained a mean (the most popular average) of 15.9 for the girls and a mean of 15.1 for the boys. In this case, the 0.8-point difference in favor of the girls is "real" because *all* boys and girls were tested. The research team did not need to conduct a significance test to help them determine whether the 0.8-point difference was due to studying just a random sample of girls, which might not be representative of all girls, and a random sample of boys, which might not be representative of all boys. (Remember that the function of significance testing is to help researchers evaluate the role of chance errors due to sampling.)

**Example C.2**

*Example of sampling errors when in truth there is no difference between groups*:

A different team of researchers conducted the same study with the same test at about the same time as the research team in Example C.1. (They did not know the other team was conducting a population study.) This second team drew a random sample of 30 tenth-grade girls and 30 tenth-grade boys and obtained a mean of 16.2 for the girls and a mean of 14.9 for the boys. Why didn't they obtain the same values as the first research team? Obviously, it is because this research team sampled. Hence, the difference in results between the two studies is due to the *sampling errors* in this study.

In practice, typically only one study is conducted using random samples. If researchers are comparing the means for two groups, there will almost always be at least a small difference (and sometimes a large difference). In either case, it is conventional for quantitative researchers to conduct a significance test, which yields a probability that the difference between the means is due to sampling errors. If there is a low probability that sampling errors created the difference (such as less than 5 out of 100 or $p < .05$), then the researchers will conclude that the difference is due to something other than chance. Such a difference is called a *statistically significant difference*.

*The Limitations of Significance Testing*

There are three major limitations to significance testing. Without knowing them, those who conduct and evaluate the results of quantitative research are likely to be misled.

First, *a significant difference can be large or small*. While it is true that larger differences tend to be statistically significant, significance tests are built on a combination of factors that can offset each other.[1] Under certain common circumstances, small differences are statistically significant. Therefore, the first limitation of significance testing is that it does not tell us whether a difference (or relationship) is large or small. (Remember that small differences can be "real" [see Example C.1], and these can be detected by significance tests.) The obvious implication for those who are evaluating research reports is that they need to consider the magnitude of any significant differences that are reported. For instance, for the difference between two means, ask "By *how many points* do the two groups differ?" and "Is this a large difference?"

The second limitation of significance testing is that a significance test does not indicate whether the result is of practical significance. For instance, a school district might have to spend millions of dollars to purchase computer-assisted instructional

---

[1] If the difference between two means is being tested for statistical significance, three factors are combined mathematically to determine the probability: the size of the difference, the size of the sample, and the amount of variation within each group. One or two of these factors can offset the other(s). For this reason, sometimes small differences are statistically significant, and sometimes large differences are *not* statistically significant.

software to get a statistically significant improvement (which might be indicated by a research report). If there are tight budgetary limits, the results of the research would be of no practical significance to the district. When considering practical significance, the most common criteria are: 1) cost in relation to benefit of a statistically significant improvement (e.g., how many points of improvement in mathematics achievement can we expect for each dollar spent?), 2) the political acceptability of an action based on a statistically significant research result (e.g., will local politicians and groups that influence them such as parents approve of the action?), and 3) the ethical and legal status of any action that might be suggested by statistically significant results.

The third limitation is that statistical significance tests are designed to assess only sampling error (errors due to random sampling). More often than not, research published in academic journals is based on samples that are clearly not drawn at random (e.g., using students in a professor's class as research participants or using volunteers). Strictly speaking, there are no significance tests appropriate for testing differences when nonrandom samples are used. Nevertheless, quantitative researchers routinely apply significance tests to such samples. As a consequence, consumers of research should consider the results of such tests as providing only tenuous information.

*Concluding Comment*

Significance testing has an important role in quantitative research when differences are being assessed in light of sampling error (i.e., chance error). If researchers are trying to show that there is a real difference (when using random samples), their first hurdle is to use statistics (including the laws of probability) to show that the difference is statistically significant. If they pass this hurdle, they should then consider how large the difference is in absolute terms (e.g., 100 points on College Boards versus 10 points on College Boards). Then, they should evaluate the practical significance of the result. If they used nonrandom samples, any conclusions regarding significance (the first hurdle) should be considered highly tenuous.

Because many researchers are more highly trained in their content areas than in statistical methods, it is not surprising that some make the mistake of assuming that when they have statistically significant results, by definition they have "important" results and discuss their results accordingly. As a savvy consumer of research, you will know to consider the absolute size of any differences as well as the practical significance of the results when evaluating their research.

*Notes*:

# Appendix D

# Detailed Description of Qualitative Data Analysis

Data analysis was based on the grounded theory method of Strauss and Corbin (1998) and followed a procedure similar to that of Richie et al. (1997). Interviews were transcribed by members of the research team, checked and corrected by the interviewer, and then sent to participants for approval or for adding of new information, giving participants the opportunity to further participate in the research (Strauss & Corbin, 1998); 2 participants chose to make additional comments.

Data analysis involved coding at four different levels. In Level I open coding, the transcripts were broken down into small, discrete parts (e.g., a word, phrase, or group of sentences), labeled as *concepts* (Strauss & Corbin, 1998). Concepts were generated from each transcript by two team members, with dyads designed to reduce researcher bias and enhance data interpretation; one member was naive about the established literature and the other more knowledgeable (cf. Richie et al., 1997), and one was Latina and the other non-Latina. Each dyad member developed concepts individually, then met with her partner to finalize wording and content of concepts. The entire research team arbitrated any unsolved disagreements, and concepts were checked against transcripts to ensure that no concepts were omitted. The use of dyads and a series of "checks," ensuring that several members of the research team reached similar conclusions, were used to enhance data analysis dependability and confirmability (Lincoln & Guba, 1985), and therefore, the investigation's trustworthiness (Miles & Huberman, 1994). The process of open coding resulted in over 3,600 concepts from the 670 single-spaced pages of raw data.

Level II coding involved the creation of *categories,* higher order labels that encompass several concepts (Strauss & Corbin, 1998). Each team member developed sets of categories from the generated concepts of all transcripts, which were compared and further synthesized by the team into one master category list, with all 3,600-plus concepts being represented. The categories were further understood by describing them in terms of properties (the characteristics of a category) and dimensions (the location of a property along a continuum) (Strauss & Corbin, 1998). For example, a property for the category labeled *mother* was "mother as influence," and was dimensionalized on a continuum of *great influence* to *little/no influence,* with each participant placed along the continuum. Properties and dimensions were generated by the primary researcher and were substantiated by the other five research team members, who reviewed the original transcripts to locate confirming or disconfirming data for each property and dimension. When all properties and dimensions were generated and reviewed, categories were tested for saturation. Saturation occurred when data analysis no longer produced new categories and when the generated categories were inclusive and descriptive of at least 80% of the participants (*n* = 18). This ensured that the categories were a true reflection of the general experiences of the Latinas in this study and could subsequently be combined in creating higher-order categories and yet preserved the atypical experiences of some participants as well. This process yielded 80 distinct categories.

The purpose of Level III axial coding was to create *key categories* (Strauss & Corbin, 1998) representing a higher level abstraction of the meaning of and relationship among the categories, generated as follows: (a) each research team member produced a list of key categories derived from the 80 categories that defined her understanding of the relations among categories; (b) the six key category lists were compared, contrasted, and discussed until a master key category list was created by team consensus; (c) properties and dimensions for key categories were generated by the primary researcher and substantiated by team members; (d) key categories were revised by the research team until saturated (Strauss & Corbin, 1998). At the key-category level, it was decided that saturation would be reached if analysis of the data did not produce any new key categories and if 100% of the women ($n = 20$) were represented by each generated key category. Because key categories were to be used in the actual construction of theory, this decision ensured that the emerging theory would be representative of all the women in the present investigation. This process yielded 14 key categories.

The emergent theory was articulated at Level IV *selective* coding. This process involved "selecting the core category, systematically relating it to other categories, validating those relationships, and filling in categories that need further refinement and development" (Strauss & Corbin, 1998, p. 116). From all key categories, one core category was chosen by team consensus to describe the essence of what emerged from the data (Strauss & Corbin, 1998). The emerging theory then was generated by analyzing the core category (i.e., developing properties and dimensions of the core category generated by the primary researcher and substantiated by research team members) and by articulating how all other key categories were related to the core category. Theory was developed by team members sharing and discussing their conceptualizations of the emerging theory. Confirming and disconfirming incidents from each original transcript were discussed and noted, referred to as negative case analysis (Lincoln & Guba, 1985). After extensive discussion and integration of team members' conceptualizations, a theoretical framework consisting of 14 key categories and judged to be inclusive of all participants' experiences was chosen as the basis for the emerging theory. By team consensus, this model was further condensed for descriptive ease by grouping the 14 key categories into four megacategories, or constructs, organized around a core category. Because the core category, constructs, key categories, categories, and concepts originated directly in the data, this emergent model represents a "grounded theory" (Strauss & Corbin, 1998).

In the final phase of data analysis, participants were sent a draft of the manuscript being prepared for publication to solicit feedback regarding accuracy, usefulness of the model in describing their experience, and protection of their identities. This process, termed *member checking,* is used to verify credibility of data analysis (a form of trustworthiness; Lincoln & Guba, 1985). Comments from the four participants who responded were incorporated into the final manuscript as appropriate.

## References

Lincoln, Y. S., & Guba, G. S. (1985). *Naturalistic inquiry.* Beverly Hills, CA: Sage.

Miles, M. B., & Huberman, A. M. (1994). *Qualitative data analysis: An expanded sourcebook* (2nd ed.). Thousand Oaks, CA: Sage.

Richie, B. S., Fassinger, R. E., Linn, S. G., Johnson, J., Prosser, J., & Robinson, S. (1997). Persistence, connection, and passion: A qualitative study of the career development of highly achieving African American–Black and White women. *Journal of Counseling Psychology, 44,* 133–148.

Strauss, A. L., & Corbin, J. (1998). *Basics of qualitative research: Techniques and procedures for developing grounded theory* (2nd ed.). Newbury Park, CA: Sage.

# Appendix E

# Checklist of Evaluation Questions

Below are the evaluation questions presented in Chapters 2 through 13 of this book. You may find it helpful to duplicate this appendix for use when evaluating research reports. Limited permission to do so is given on page *ii* of this book. Keep in mind that your professor may require you to justify each of your responses.

## Chapter 2 Evaluating Titles

____ 1. Is the title sufficiently specific?

____ 2. Is the title reasonably concise?

____ 3. Are the primary variables referred to in the title?

____ 4. Does the title identify the types of individuals who participated?

____ 5. If a study is strongly tied to a theory, is the name of the specific theory mentioned in the title?

____ 6. Does the title indicate the nature of the research without describing the results?

____ 7. Has the author avoided using a "yes–no" question as a title?

____ 8. If there is a main title and a subtitle, do both provide important information about the research?

____ 9. If the title implies causality, does the method of research justify it?

____ 10. Is the title free of jargon and acronyms that might be unknown to the audience for the research report?

____ 11. Overall, is the title effective and appropriate?

## Chapter 3   Evaluating Abstracts

____ 1. Is the purpose of the study referred to or at least clearly implied?

____ 2. Does the abstract highlight the research methodology?

____ 3. Has the researcher omitted the titles of measures (except when these are the focus of the research)?

____ 4. Are the highlights of the results described?

____ 5. If the study is strongly tied to a theory, is the theory mentioned in the abstract?

____ 6. Has the researcher avoided making vague references to implications and future research directions?

____ 7. Overall, is the abstract effective and appropriate?

## Chapter 4   Evaluating Introductions and Literature Reviews

____ 1. Does the researcher begin by identifying a specific problem area?

____ 2. Does the researcher establish the importance of the problem area?

____ 3. Are any underlying theories adequately described?

____ 4. Does the Introduction move from topic to topic instead of from citation to citation?

____ 5. Is the Introduction a coherent essay with logical transitions from topic to topic?

____ 6. Has the researcher provided conceptual definitions of key terms?

____ 7. Has the researcher indicated the basis for "factual" statements?

____ 8. Do the specific research purposes, questions, or hypotheses logically flow from the introductory material?

____ 9. Overall, is the Introduction effective and appropriate?

## Chapter 5   A Closer Look at Evaluating Literature Reviews

_____ 1. If there is extensive literature on a topic, has the researcher been selective?

_____ 2. Is the literature review critical?

_____ 3. Is current research cited?

_____ 4. Has the researcher distinguished between opinions and research findings?

_____ 5. Has the researcher distinguished between what is proposed by a theory and research findings related to the theory?

_____ 6. Has the researcher interpreted research literature in light of the inherent limits of empirical research?

_____ 7. Has the researcher avoided the overuse of direct quotations from the literature?

_____ 8. Overall, is the literature review portion of the Introduction appropriate?

## Chapter 6   Evaluating Samples When Researchers Generalize

_____ 1. Was random sampling used?

_____ 2. If random sampling was used, was it stratified?

_____ 3. If the randomness of a sample is impaired by the refusal to participate by some of those selected, is the rate of participation reasonably high?

_____ 4. If the randomness of a sample is impaired by the refusal to participate by some of those selected, is there reason to believe that the participants and nonparticipants are similar on relevant variables?

_____ 5. If a sample from which a researcher wants to generalize was not selected at random, is it at least drawn from the target group for the generalization?

_____ 6. If a sample from which a researcher wants to generalize was not selected at random, is it at least reasonably diverse?

_____ 7. If a sample from which a researcher wants to generalize was not selected at random, does the researcher explicitly discuss this limitation?

\_\_\_ 8. Has the author described relevant demographics of the sample?

\_\_\_ 9. Is the overall size of the sample adequate?

\_\_\_ 10. Is the number of participants in each group sufficiently large?

\_\_\_ 11. Has informed consent been obtained?

\_\_\_ 12. Overall, is the sample appropriate for generalizing?

## Chapter 7   Evaluating Samples When Researchers Do *Not* Generalize

\_\_\_ 1. Has the researcher described the sample/population in sufficient detail?

\_\_\_ 2. For a pilot study or developmental test of a theory, has the researcher used a sample with relevant demographics?

\_\_\_ 3. Even if the purpose is not to generalize to a population, has the researcher used a sample of adequate size?

\_\_\_ 4. If a purposive sample has been used, has the researcher indicated the basis for selecting individuals to include?

\_\_\_ 5. If a population has been studied, has it been clearly identified and described?

\_\_\_ 6. Has informed consent been obtained?

\_\_\_ 7. Overall, is the description of the sample adequate?

## Chapter 8   Evaluating Instrumentation

\_\_\_ 1. Have the actual items and questions (or at least a sample of them) been provided?

\_\_\_ 2. Are any specialized response formats, settings, and/or restrictions described in detail?

\_\_\_ 3. When appropriate, are multiple methods used to collect data/information on each variable?

\_\_\_ 4. For published instruments, have sources where additional information can be obtained been cited?

_____ 5. When delving into sensitive matters, is there reason to believe that accurate data were obtained?

_____ 6. Have steps been taken to keep the instrumentation from obtruding on and changing any overt behaviors that were observed?

_____ 7. If the collection and coding of observations is highly subjective, is there evidence that similar results would be obtained if another researcher used the same measurement techniques with the same group at the same time?

_____ 8. If an instrument is designed to measure a single unitary trait, does it have adequate internal consistency?

_____ 9. For stable traits, is there evidence of temporal stability?

_____ 10. When appropriate, is there evidence of content validity?

_____ 11. When appropriate, is there evidence of empirical validity?

_____ 12. Do the researchers discuss obvious limitations of their instrumentation?

_____ 13. Overall, is the instrumentation adequate?

## Chapter 9   Evaluating Experimental Procedures

_____ 1. If two or more groups are compared, were individuals assigned at random to the groups?

_____ 2. If two or more comparison groups were _not_ formed at random, is there evidence that they were initially equal in important ways?

_____ 3. If only a single participant or a single group is used, have the treatments been alternated?

_____ 4. Are the treatments described in sufficient detail?

_____ 5. If the treatments were administered by individuals other than the researcher, were they properly trained?

_____ 6. If the treatments were administered by individuals other than the researcher, was there a check to see if they administered the treatments properly?

___ 7. If each treatment group had a different person administering a treatment, has the researcher tried to eliminate the "personal effect"?

___ 8. Except for differences in the treatments, were all other conditions the same in the experimental and control groups?

___ 9. When appropriate, have the researchers considered possible "demand characteristics"?

___ 10. Is the setting for the experiment "natural"?

___ 11. Has the researcher distinguished between *random selection* and *random assignment*?

___ 12. Has the researcher used ethical and politically acceptable treatments?

___ 13. Overall, was the experiment properly conducted?

## Chapter 10   Evaluating Analysis and Results Sections: Quantitative Research

___ 1. Have appropriate descriptive statistics been reported?

___ 2. If any differences are statistically significant and small, have the researchers noted that they are small?

___ 3. Is the Results section a cohesive essay?

___ 4. Does the researcher refer back to the research hypotheses, purposes, or questions originally stated in the Introduction?

___ 5. When there are a number of related statistics, have they been presented in a table?

___ 6. If there are tables, are their highlights discussed in the narrative of the Results section?

___ 7. Have the researchers presented descriptive statistics before presenting the results of inferential tests?

___ 8. Overall, is the presentation of the results comprehensible?

____   9. Overall, is the presentation of the results adequate?

## Chapter 11   Evaluating Analysis and Results Sections: Qualitative Research

____   1. Were the data analyzed independently by two or more individuals?

____   2. Did the researchers seek feedback from experienced individuals and auditors before finalizing the results?

____   3. Did the researchers seek feedback from the participants (i.e., use member checking) before finalizing the results?

____   4. Did the researchers name the method of analysis they used and provide (a) reference(s) for it?

____   5. Do the researchers state *specifically* how the method of analysis was applied?

____   6. Are the Results of *qualitative* studies adequately supported with examples of quotations or descriptions of observations?

____   7. When appropriate, are statistics reported (especially for demographic data)?

____   8. Overall, is the Results section clearly organized?

____   9. Overall, is the presentation of the results adequate?

## Chapter 12   Evaluating Discussion Sections

____   1. In long articles, do the researchers briefly summarize the purpose and results at the beginning of the Discussion?

____   2. Do the researchers acknowledge specific methodological limitations?

____   3. Are the results discussed in terms of the literature cited in the Introduction?

____   4. Have the researchers avoided citing new references in the Discussion?

____   5. Are specific implications discussed?

____ 6. Are the results discussed in terms of any relevant theories?

____ 7. Are suggestions for future research specific?

____ 8. Have the researchers distinguished between speculation and data-based conclusions?

____ 9. Overall, is the Discussion effective and appropriate?

## Chapter 13   Putting It All Together

____ 1. In your judgment, have the researchers selected an important problem?

____ 2. Were the researchers reflective?

____ 3. Is the report cohesive?

____ 4. Does the report extend the boundaries of our knowledge on a topic, especially our understanding of relevant theories?

____ 5. Are any major methodological flaws unavoidable or forgivable?

____ 6. Is the research likely to inspire additional research?

____ 7. Is the research likely to help in decision making?

____ 8. All things considered, is the report worthy of publication in an academic journal?

____ 9. Would you be proud to have your name on the research article as a co-author?

*Notes:*

*Notes*: